Date Due

NOV 27			
NOV 21			
7-16-79			
11-8-2004			

PATRIOT DOCTOR

The Story of Benjamin Rush

BORN: JANUARY 4, 1746
DIED: APRIL 19, 1813

PATRIOT DOCTOR

The Story of Benjamin Rush

★ ★ ★ ★ ★ ★ ★ ★ ★ ★ ★ ★ ★

BY ESTHER M. DOUTY

13059

Julian Messner, Inc · New York

Published by Julian Messner, Inc.
8 West 40 Street, New York 18

Published simultaneously in Canada
by The Copp Clark Publishing Co. Limited

Printed in the United States of America

Library of Congress Catalog Card No. 59-12757

For H. M. D.

Acknowledgments

To

Sergeant Elsie Davis of the Medical Museum, Armed Forces Institute, Washington, D.C.

Miss Julia Harty of the Rare Book Room, The Library of Congress, Washington, D.C.

The Library Staff of the Medical School of the University of Edinburgh, Edinburgh, Scotland

The Library Staff of the National Library of Medicine, Washington, D.C.

Dr. W. B. McDaniel, 2nd, Curator of the Historical Collections of the College of Physicians of Philadelphia

Miss Eilidh McInnes, A.B., Archivist of St. Thomas Hospital, London, England

Mrs. Ella N. Wade, Curator of the Museum of the College of Physicians of Philadelphia

for their helpful interest in providing me with special material needed for this book, and to Dr. John H. Powell of Philadelphia, whose wise suggestions and inspired approach to history first brought Dr. Benjamin Rush to my attention,

I give my sincerest thanks.

ESTHER M. DOUTY

Contents

Contents

PATRIOT DOCTOR

The Story of Benjamin Rush

CHAPTER ONE

The Blazing Star

Early one summer morning in 1754 a thick fog rolled in from the Delaware River and lay like a soft gray blanket over the city of Philadelphia. The fog was so heavy that eight-year-old Benjamin Rush, peering from his bedroom window over his mother's grocery shop, the Blazing Star, could not see the vast market sheds which lay directly across the street.

Although it was not yet six o'clock, he could hear his mother bustling about in the shop below, getting ready for the day's business. There was another sound too—the clank of heavy iron pans being moved about. Good, he thought. The sound meant that his sisters, thirteen-year-old Rachel and ten-year-old Rebecca, were fixing breakfast. A moment later the aroma of frying scrapple floated up the narrow stairway.

The spicy smell made Benjamin's mouth water. Just as soon as he could yank on his clothes he would dash down for food. No, he remembered, first he must stop by the wash stand and run a chalked rag over his teeth to clean them. Mama was fussy about her children's teeth.

Across the room his seven-year-old brother Jacob still slept and snuffled in their rope bed. Benjamin hurried over and poked the boy's chubby back. "Get up, Jacob," he ordered. "It's nigh on six, and Mama'll be needing us now that James has gone to sea. And don't forget to chalk your teeth before you come downstairs."

As he spoke, Benjamin slid his feet into his boots. Then he ran down the little winding stairway to the shop. At first he didn't see his mother, but soon he discovered her standing in the doorway. She was just standing there quietly—listening. As usual, she looked rosy-cheeked, bright-eyed, and alert.

"What are you listening to, Mama?" The boy's clear, high-pitched voice was curious.

Mother Rush raised one hand for silence. "Hush, Benjamin, I'm trying to hear the bell at the ferry—the one they ring on foggy days to guide the market boats to the wharf. Mr. Wick from Jersey has promised me a specially nice lot of vegetables today. Oh, I do hope this fog won't keep him away. I don't want to disappoint my customers."

"Oh, you won't disappoint them, Mama," Benjamin said quickly. "You never do."

Benjamin was right. Due to her shrewdness, energy and reliability, Mrs. Susanna Rush was making a real success of the grocery and general store she had opened three years ago— soon after her husband had died and left her with six young children to support.

The youngest child, also named John like his father, had died shortly after birth, so Benjamin couldn't remember him very well. He did, however, have a clear memory of his father as a modest, kindly, youngish man who every night gathered his children around him at the fireside and read to them from the Bible. He never had had much to say, and in this respect he was quite different from Benjamin's mother who was always bustling about, full of lively conversation and plans for the future.

Mother Rush said she had always been that way. Because of this she had been able to persuade her father, a prosperous Pennsylvania farmer, to give her a real education at a boarding school where she had studied philosophy and mathematics just as if she were a boy.

Benjamin had been told that he acted like his mother, but he looked like his father. In appearance he was well formed, on the thin side, with large, extraordinarily clear and alive blue eyes, and shining light brown hair.

Now as he stood with his mother in the doorway of the Blazing Star, a sudden clumping noise from the stairway made them both turn around. A moment later Jacob appeared, wiping his nose with the sleeve of his nightgown. It was plain that he was taking cold.

"Oh, Jacob," Mother Rush lamented. "I declare you're as sickly as James—always snuffling and coughing. If you were older, I'd send you off to sea, too, for your health. Well, let's try to head off the distemper. Benjamin, fetch Jacob his jump rope."

While she spoke, she reached for the water bucket and poured out half a tumbler of water. Next she added some rum to the water and held it out to Jacob. "Here, child, drink this. Now," she ordered as Jacob downed the amber liquid, "jump rope—fast. When you work up a real good sweat, hop back into bed and stay there till noon."

Like most mothers in the American colonies, Mother Rush considered herself a pretty good doctor. She knew all the remedies listed in Buchan's *Domestic Medicine* and in Benjamin Franklin's *The Poor Planter's Physician*, and dozens more besides.

Benjamin watched his little brother tiredly start to jump rope. Then as he himself edged toward the kitchen and breakfast, his mother stopped him. "You pay attention to what I'm saying, Benjamin," she said sharply. "You cough an awful lot yourself."

"Yes, Mama," the boy answered without enthusiasm. Sickness and its treatment bored him. He continued on his way to the smoky, low-ceilinged kitchen where the two girls, sturdy and dark haired like their mother, were already eating.

Rachel handed him a thick brown plate piled high with fried apples and slices of crispy scrapple. "Hurry and eat, Benj," she said. "Mama wants you to unpack that new barrel of crockery before she opens the shop today."

At that moment Mrs. Rush stepped into the kitchen. "No, Rachel," she said. "I've changed my mind. The fog is lifting so I want Benjamin to run down to the wharf and watch for Mr. Wick."

"And when you see him, son," Mother Rush turned her bright eyes to Benjamin, "please ask him to come directly to the Blazing Star instead of calling at the other shops first. Tell him, Benjamin, that I'll make it worth his while. Hasten now, boy. You've had enough to eat."

"All right, Mama." Benjamin gulped down a final swallow of tea.

He hurried outside into Market Street which already rumbled with the noise of heavy-wheeled produce wagons rolling over the cobblestones. Deftly he dodged across the busy street, past the great market sheds where one could buy everything from oranges to fine lace, then headed for the wharves along the Delaware.

Philadelphia's bustling waterfront always thrilled Benjamin. Often he thought that the masts of the ships anchored there looked like a vast forest of trees. And the strange sound of foreign tongues as the longshoremen unloaded the products of half the world likewise stirred him. On the streets, Benjamin heard almost every language of the civilized world. He already easily recognized French and German, especially German—a language used by so many Philadelphians that it often appeared on the street signs, printed just underneath the English.

Every day, Benjamin noticed new faces in the fast-growing city. They were strong, spirited faces whose owners were eager to begin earning a good living in this new country where the rewards from nature's treasures were reported to lie within the reach of all. No wonder that in 1754 Philadelphia with its fifteen thousand people was the greatest port and the largest, most prosperous, cultured and elegant city in all the American colonies.

But today Benjamin did not let his attention stray to the colorful crowds. He kept his eye out for Mr. Wick, a fat, jolly Quaker who, his mother declared, grew the best beans in Jersey. He was in luck because when he arrived at Jones's wharf, he saw Mr. Wick already there, transferring his vegetables to a hired cart.

"All right, lad," Mr. Wick, out of breath from lifting the loaded baskets, puffed when Benjamin had delivered his message. "I'll make directly for the Blazing Star. I'm always willing to help out a hard-working widow like your mother. Like to ride back with me?"

Benjamin would have preferred to linger at the wharves but he knew his mother needed him. He climbed up beside Mr. Wick and answered his questions absently while he watched the sun break through the clouds and glisten brightly on the pink, blue, red and yellow buildings of the fine, new, lively city.

When Mr. Wick pulled up in front of the Blazing Star, Rebecca bounced out of the doorway. "Oh, Benj," she called excitedly, "guess what? Aunt Sarah is here. I think she is going to take you away with her."

"Take me away with her!" Benjamin stared at his sister's

serious face. Then he dashed into the shop where his mother was already leaning over Mr. Wick's vegetables, inspecting them with miss-nothing eyes. She glanced up briefly. "Go speak to your Aunt Sarah, Benjamin. She's in the kitchen. I'll join you as soon as I pay Mr. Wick."

His mother certainly wasn't acting as though Aunt Sarah was going to take him away with her, Benjamin thought with relief. Nevertheless he didn't feel easy as he walked into the kitchen, where Rachel was scouring the greasy skillet with sand.

Aunt Sarah was sitting on the wooden stool by the fireplace, looking, Benjamin decided, older than his mother, although she was younger. Perhaps it was as Mother Rush often re-marked, "Sarah has too much to do—what with caring for her own eight children and seeing to the cooking and the care of all the pupils at the Academy besides."

By the Academy, Mrs. Rush meant the famous Nottingham Academy where Aunt Sarah's husband the Reverend Samuel Finley was principal. In the few years since Uncle Finley had established this school it had become one of the most famous in the colonies. Many aristocratic Philadelphia families like the Morgans and the Shippens sent their sons there, and pupils came from as far away as the Carolinas.

Every so often Benjamin wondered what it would be like to be away at school with a lot of other boys instead of taking lessons from his mother. Right now, however, he did not have time for such thoughts, for Aunt Sarah was smiling and holding out her hand to him. Benjamin took her hand and bowed politely. Then his aunt drew him close.

"In truth, you are a fine-looking lad, Benjamin," she said warmly. "Sincerity shines from every feature of your face. It will be a pleasure to have you with us at Nottingham."

"Me at Nottingham?" Benjamin exclaimed in dismay. "I can't leave here. What will Mama do without me now that James has gone to sea?"

"Don't you worry about that, son," Mother Rush said emphatically as she stepped into the kitchen. "The girls and I will make out. You, and Jacob, too, need a man's guidance—and more schooling than I can give you. We are indeed fortunate that Uncle Finley is willing to accept you at the Academy as nonpaying pupils."

"Think nothing of it, Susanna," Aunt Sarah interrupted gently. "You know that Reverend Finley feels that in educating your fatherless boys, he is only doing his Christian duty."

"Only doing his Christian duty."

Somehow, thought Benjamin, that didn't have a very friendly sound. But he saw that his mother was pleased with the idea, so he kept his misgivings to himself.

Before Aunt Sarah left, it was decided that Benjamin and Jacob would come to Nottingham for the new term which was to begin in August. This delay gave the boys time to get used to the idea of going away to school, and soon they even began looking forward to it.

On the morning of departure they waited at the stage depot with unusually shining and rosy faces. Just yesterday Mama had taken them to the Public Bath House where they scrubbed really clean in a hot, allover bath. Such a bath was a rare experience and Benjamin realized what an important occasion going away to school was.

About eight o'clock the stagecoach driver flicked his whip over the backs of the horses, and the heavy coach rumbled away over the cobblestones. Benjamin leaned out of the window and waved good-by to his mother and sisters, who stood with bright stiff smiles for as long as he could see them.

It took the stage nearly three days and several changes of horses to rock and bump the sixty miles to the village of Rising Sun, Maryland, where the Academy was located. In the village the boys found Casp, the Academy handy man, waiting for them with a wagon. As Casp stowed away their luggage, Benjamin noticed the odd glance he gave their fishing poles and rifles. Benjamin was proud of these fine Pennsylvania German rifles. They had been given to him and Jacob by Mr. Richard Morris, the distiller, a friend of their mother's, who often took them hunting in some nearby woods.

"Up ye go, lads," said Casp as he hoisted them to the wide board seat of the wagon. A moment later they were bumping along a dusty, rutty road which ran through low, wooded hills. Soon the wagon creaked to a stop in front of a large white-columned mansion.

"Here we be," said Casp. "And there be the Reverend Finley waitin' fer ye."

As he spoke, a short, chubby, pink-cheeked, jolly-looking man of forty hastened down the broad steps to greet them. "Welcome, Benjamin. Welcome, Jacob," he called in a friendly voice which carried the Scottish burr of his North Ireland birthplace. "Your Aunt Sarah and I are indeed pleased that you are joining our family."

Then Uncle Finley noticed the fishing poles and the rifles. "Pray, what are those for?" he demanded, the jolliness fading from his voice.

"Why, sir, they are for hunting and fishing," Benjamin answered, puzzled by his uncle's manner. "Mr. Morris said the woods and streams hereabouts abound with game and fish."

"And so they do," Uncle Finley agreed. "But our pupils do not need to hunt and fish for food. And to hunt and fish for pleasure smacks of idleness. And idleness, lads," the school principal paused impressively, "is almost a sin. In my view," he went on, "a boy should never be idle but should be occupied in useful activity every waking moment of his day. When he is not engaged in actual labor, his mind should be absorbing useful knowledge from the people and surroundings about him —just as a plant continually absorbs nourishment from its environment. Do you understand, Benjamin?" he asked urgently. "And you, Jacob?"

Jacob merely nodded, but Benjamin, his large eyes thoughtful, said, "Yes, Uncle, I understand." All at once he felt he had learned something valuable.

CHAPTER TWO

Uncle Finley

As a scholar the Reverend Finley taught Latin, Greek, philosophy, mathematics and composition to the thirty pupils at Nottingham. As a Presbyterian minister he imparted "special instruction for their souls."

Thus for five years—until he was fourteen—Benjamin Rush listened to Uncle Finley begin and end each day by reading and explaining some part of the Bible. And on Sunday nights, like the other students, he repeated as much as he could remember of the sermons he had heard at church that day.

At these sermon-repeating sessions, Benjamin always had the most to say. He had a good memory, and he knew it. In fact Benjamin secretly believed that he had the best memory at the Academy, although he was sure that shrewd-eyed Ebenezer Hazard would dispute his claim.

One Wednesday afternoon, as he and Ebenezer and several of the older students were cutting hay in the Academy hayfield, Ebenezer remarked, "Hay certainly cannot have much phlogiston in it. It is so light. Yet it burns readily. How do you explain that?"

Benjamin turned his brilliant blue eyes on him. "Phlogiston has no weight at all," he announced in a positive tone. "It has no color, odor, taste or weight. So the fact that hay does burn readily shows that it has a great deal of phlogiston in it, Ebenezer."

With a smug expression on his face, Benjamin went back to his raking. He did not observe the meaningful look that passed between Ebenezer and the other students, nor did he notice that Uncle Finley was standing within earshot under a peach tree.

Since it was Wednesday Benjamin was looking forward to the evening meal, for at Wednesday suppers Uncle Finley told stories. Usually the stories dealt with great heroes of the past, but every so often the Reverend Finley would make up tales about Riverby Academy and its "noblest student—Johnny Courtly."

"Johnny Courtly," Uncle Finley explained, "was an example of all that was proper and amiable in the conduct of a young man, while the other students, such as Bill Slovenly, Timothy Rude-Boy, and the like—well, they definitely needed improvement." When he wanted to, Uncle Finley could be very funny, and the boys always knew which Nottingham student he had in mind as he spun his Riverby tales.

This night as Benjamin spooned up his bread pudding, he heard his uncle say, "Lads, did I ever tell you about a pupil at Riverby named Cecil Know-It-All?"

Benjamin laid down his spoon and prepared to listen with enjoyment. Then all at once little prickles raced up his spine. For years he had known that his uncle was an excellent play actor who could sound like anyone he chose to. And now, he asked himself unhappily, who was it that Uncle Finley sounded like in the role of Cecil Know-It-All?

Benjamin felt uncomfortably hot. In the candlelight his cheeks flamed scarlet. Across the table he could see Ebenezer's mocking smile. He dared not look at anyone else. Surely even the youngest grinning pupil was aware that Cecil Know-It-All,

with his precise, positive tone of voice, and Benjamin Rush
were one and the same.

At last the horrible meal was over. The boys drifted off to
the common room still chuckling over Cecil Know-It-All's
downfall. Benjamin slunk outside to the wide porch to cool his
heated cheeks. In a few minutes Uncle Finley stepped out on
the porch and gazed quietly up at the stars. Benjamin drew a
deep breath and went over to him.

"Uncle Finley," he began unhappily, "I do not understand
what you meant by Cecil Know-It-All. I was right about the
phlogiston—and about the other things, too."

"I know you were right, Benjamin," his uncle said under-
standingly. "Indeed you have learned many facts in your thirteen years. But there is something else you must learn—humility.
Knowledge without humility, Benjamin, will bring you enemies." With that, Uncle Finley patted Ben's arm and went
back into the candlelit common room, leaving a puzzled and
unhappy boy behind him.

Nearly a year later, in the spring of 1759, on a Saturday just
before evening prayers, Uncle Finley called Benjamin into the
little sitting room which he used for his own family. Benjamin
noticed Aunt Sarah leaning back in the wing chair by the
window and staring silently out at the gathering dusk. At the
boy's greeting, she smiled wanly and then went back to her
quiet dreaming. Benjamin felt a tug at his heart. How utterly
weary Aunt Sarah appeared these days. Even though she sipped
strengthening wines at tea and at dinner and drank the water
in which rusted nails had lain, no sparkle showed in her deep-
circled eyes.

In contrast to his wife, Uncle Finley was, as usual, lively as a puppy. "Sit down, Benjamin," he commanded. "I want to talk to you about your future."

"My future, Uncle?" Benjamin echoed uneasily.

Having to talk about his future with Uncle Finley made Benjamin uneasy chiefly because he had no idea what he wanted to do. He realized that many boys of fourteen knew they wanted to be preachers, or lawyers, or doctors, or sea captains, rich merchants or plantation owners, but he himself felt no great interest in any one calling. Or rather he was interested in them all—except perhaps physic. He preferred to spend his time with healthy people—not with sick ones.

But now Uncle Finley was saying, "Yes, Benjamin, after thinking the matter over, I feel definitely that you have learned all I can teach you here. All I can teach you scholastically, that is," he amended. "There is nothing to be gained by your staying here longer. I am sure you are ready for the College of New Jersey, perhaps even for one of the upper classes."

In the American colonies in those days a boy could enter college as soon as he passed certain academic tests. It didn't matter if he was twelve years old or twenty; if he had been to a preparatory school or had been tutored at home; if he could pass the entrance examinations and had satisfactory character references, he was "in." So Benjamin wasn't surprised that his uncle considered him ready for college. He wasn't sure, however, that Mama could pay for his expenses.

Uncle Finley seemed to read his thoughts. "You need not worry about the ninety dollars a year that the college will cost, Benjamin," he remarked. "Now that your mother is wed to Mr. Morris, she is quite well fixed financially. She can easily pay for your further education with the handsome sum she received when she sold the Blazing Star. Suppose you plan to leave for the college in a fortnight, lad."

So far as Uncle Finley was concerned, the matter was settled. He stood up and dismissed his nephew with a bow.

Thus it happened that on a drizzly day two weeks later Benjamin Rush was seated in the stage bound for the College of New Jersey. By the time the coach pulled up at the depot in the village of Princeton, however, the weather had turned crisp and clear. As soon as the boy alighted, he hurried up the spring-damp street to the great gray building called Nassau Hall which, he had heard, was the largest stone edifice in the colonies.

Within this building, Benjamin knew, the tutors were waiting to find out if he knew enough Latin and Greek, geography and logic, rhetoric and mathematics to enter the college.

At first Benjamin was frightened at being examined by two black-robed men with great curled wigs and unsmiling faces. But aided by kindly promptings from Tutor Halsey, he soon calmed down. In the end he did so well that he was admitted to the Junior Class.

As he hastened from the examination room on swift, light feet, Mr. Halsey called, "Now that your ordeal is over, Rush, would you like to see the college library?"

"Indeed I would, sir," Benjamin answered eagerly. Like many colonials he thought of books as precious things, almost like silver or gold.

At the top of the broad staircase on the second floor, Mr. Halsey opened the door to a large, sunny room smelling of old leather. "Here we are," he announced proudly, "twelve hundred books—and every one a gift from some friend of colonial education, either in the provinces or in Europe. Of course," he went on in an apologetic tone, "since they were donated, they are usually not the newest things on the subject. But—

well, we try all the time to collect more volumes. I plan myself to go abroad after this term, and beg books from every clergyman in Scotland."

Benjamin's eyes were on the five students who sat at a large table studying. One of them raised sharp gray eyes and grinned.

"Why," Benjamin exclaimed as he recognized the grin, "it's Ebenezer Hazard! I knew him at Nottingham."

"Well, then," Tutor Halsey beckoned to Ebenezer, "he's the very one to show you about the college. Hazard, suppose you take over and help Rush through his first days here."

Ebenezer (years later to become Postmaster General of the United States) was a good choice for this job. He had already been at Princeton a year and knew all the ninety students there. Like Benjamin, he was interested in everything.

Right now it was food. "Let's go round to the Buttery," he suggested, "and have a kidney pie and a small beer."

On the way out of Nassau Hall Benjamin peered into the spacious, white-painted assembly room with its enormous portraits of George II and Belcher, the Royal Governor.

"That is where you have to be careful," Ebenezer muttered. "They watch you like a hawk in there."

"They do?"

"They do indeed," Ebenezer warned. "Decorum. That is the thing to mind. Keep your hat off for ten rods in the President's presence, and for five in the tutor's. Do not speak loudly in the presence of your superiors, and do not speak to anyone from a distance. And never use nicknames, Ben—I mean, Benjamin."

"Those are but small things," said Benjamin.

"To be sure," Ebenezer agreed, "there is also drunkenness, lying and theft. If you are called up for these, you either make a public confession before the whole college or you are expelled.

If you frequent a tavern or a place of public entertainment, or associate with those known to lead scandalous lives, you are expelled. And if you fight or are absent from prayers, you are fined."

"I see," Benjamin looked unconcerned. Actually he couldn't imagine himself committing any of these misdeeds.

Just then Ebenezer grabbed his arm. "There's the President. Quick—off with your hat. And bow—low."

But the boys' curtsy went unnoticed, for in the distance Reverend Jacob Green turned off on a side path. Green was officially only "acting" president. He had been named in an emergency to take the place of President Jonathan Edwards who had died of a smallpox inoculation just five weeks after his inauguration. Several months later Green was succeeded by a thirty-six-year-old minister from Virginia named Samuel Davies.

The choice of Reverend Davies came to mean a great deal to Benjamin Rush, for Davies had new and different ideas about what was important to a college student. Unlike most college presidents of the time, he did not think that a knowledge of Latin and Greek was all important. And perhaps because he was himself a noted pulpit orator, he believed that public speaking and composition were the subjects which would mean most to a young man in later life.

With this thought in mind, Davies introduced a "weekly course of disputation" in which the students debated with their classmates. And once a month on "monthly oration day" each student presented a "harangue of his own composition" before the college and the congregation of the Presbyterian church in Princeton. These orations were then criticized from the standpoint of delivery and effective and accurate writing.

It was in these two subjects—the public "harangues" and

composition—that Benjamin excelled. The first time he stood on the Assembly Hall stage and "harangued," President Davies leaned forward, fascinated.

"Who is that pupil?" he asked Tutor Ewing.

"Benjamin Rush of Philadelphia, sir."

"His delivery is remarkable—so clear—and what he says so full of sense and logic. I must give him my personal attention."

After that, although Benjamin continued with mathematics, and passed through courses of natural and moral philosophy, metaphysics, chronology and more Latin and Greek, his attention was given chiefly to public speaking and to writing.

President Davies also impressed him with the importance of keeping a notebook, or Commonplace Book, as it was called then.

"A good notebook, Rush," declared Davies one day, "should contain passages from any book you find worthwhile. It should also contain important opinions or unusual facts which you have heard in lectures or in conversations. And alongside the passages you have entered, you should inscribe your opinion of them. This practice will develop your own powers of analysis and expression."

Benjamin Rush was fifteen when he began his first Commonplace Book. Throughout his life he kept many such notebooks. It was to this custom that he later ascribed his ability to turn out an amazing number of books and pamphlets upon a variety of subjects.

The months at Princeton sped by. There were happy evenings when Benjamin sat before the great fireplace in the common room, cracking walnuts and roasting apples, "disputing" all the while with the other students. There was also the black day when he got that letter from his mother. "Your dear Aunt

Sarah," the letter had read, "died Thursday last—of woman trouble."

On the third Wednesday in August, 1760, fifteen-year-old Benjamin Rush awoke to the sound of the warning bell for daily morning prayers. He would have to hurry if he was to get to the services on time—six o'clock. Well, he thought sleepily, this will be the last time—if I pass the Public Examinations this afternoon.

Benjamin, like the other four seniors, was worried at the prospect of being publicly examined, not only by all the professors and the college trustees, but by any gentlemen of learning in the colonies who wished to question them. But as it turned out, the seniors were lucky this year. Not a single strange gentleman of learning appeared, the trustees were silent, and the professors asked only questions which seniors had been asked for years. All five passed and were told to prepare to receive their Bachelor of Arts degree at the Commencement exercises in September.

At these exercises, each graduate gave a speech. The first two spoke in Latin. "The third, Mr. Benjamin Rush," according to the newspapers, "in a very sprightly and entertaining manner delivered an ingenious English harangue in Praise of Oratory."

When the exercises were over, the families and friends of the graduates streamed outside Nassau Hall into the moonlit evening. Benjamin, hunting his mother and Jacob, joined the throng. Suddenly a little girl, lost in the crowd, fell into his path. She was frightened and crying. Benjamin picked her up and smoothed the tousled brown curls back from her face.

"Do not cry, my poppet," he comforted her. "We shall find your mama. What is your name?"

"She is Julia Stockton," someone answered from the crowd. "Mayhap you had better take her home."

Everybody in Princeton knew where the Stocktons lived— in a beautiful mansion called Morven not far from the college. With hurried steps, Ben carried little Julia to Morven and handed her to a servant. Then he ran back to the college to find his own family.

Before he left for Philadelphia, Benjamin went to President Davies' study to bid him good-by. The President stood up and extended a friendly hand.

"Well, Rush, so now you are setting sail upon the sea of Life. I wish you every success. By the way, have you decided upon the profession you intend to follow?"

"Yes, sir, I have," answered Benjamin with enthusiasm, pleased that at last he knew what he wanted to do. "I intend the study of the law."

"The law! Excellent," exclaimed Davies. "With your powerful way of speaking and your skill in argument, I should say you were born for that profession. Yes, born for it," he repeated.

Back in Philadelphia, his mother also thought Ben would make a fine lawyer. With her usual energy, she made arrangements for him to read law in the office of a good lawyer she knew.

A short time before Benjamin actually signed up with the lawyer, he visited a classmate in Maryland. On the way back to Philadelphia, he stopped off to see Uncle Finley at Nottingham. His uncle, looking less pink cheeked and thinner since Aunt Sarah's death, was happy to see him. "Come in, Benjamin, come in. I hear you made a fine record at college, and we are all proud of you."

For an hour they talked about all kinds of things. Then Uncle Finley fixed a firm glance on his nephew and said, "Tell me, Benjamin, have you decided upon your life's work?"

"Yes, sir," answered the boy, glowing happily in the light of his uncle's praise. "I am going to study the law."

"The law!" Uncle Finley's voice was sharp and disbelieving. "Did you say the law, Benjamin?" He stood up abruptly. "The law is full of evil temptation, lad. By no means think of it. Why not study physic?"

For a moment Benjamin could say nothing. He gazed with blank eyes at his uncle. Then his voice came back to him.

"But Uncle Finley," he protested, "I do not like physic. I—I cannot even stand the sight of blood."

"That matters not," declared his uncle in a positive tone. He stared up at his nephew with commanding dark eyes. "What does matter, Benjamin, is that 'tis with the study of physic that you will help mankind; not with the practice of the law. It is one's duty to help one's fellow man, is it not? Pray on this matter, lad. Pray on it hard, and the answer will come to you." He pressed a strong hand on Benjamin's shoulder. "Good-by, lad. May God's wisdom be with you," he said affectionately.

For a long time Benjamin Rush stood alone on the broad veranda, leaning against the white porch column and gazing vacantly at the blue haze of the distant hills.

"Oh, I know not what to do," he murmured unhappily. "Perhaps Uncle Finley is right. Perhaps I should give up reading law. But physic—purging, bleeding, cutting! Ugh." He smacked the porch column with his hand and rushed down the steps to his waiting horse.

CHAPTER THREE

Medicine—Without Science

Mile after mile of the dusty road passed under his horse's hoofs, but Benjamin rode on with unseeing eyes. His mind was a churning mass of confusion. Physic! Uncle Finley thought he should become a physician. Undoubtedly the practice of medicine was a noble calling, one which offered real opportunity to serve one's fellow man. But in his heart Benjamin felt he was meant for the law. Why else was he given that quick, argumentative turn of mind? For what other reason was he born with a love and an ability for public speaking? Why did he have a talent for persuasion, which even at fifteen was evident to many people? Besides, he told himself, he was *interested* in the law.

But there was Uncle Finley—a fine man, a true man of God, who had been almost a father to him these past six years. Long ago he had taken Uncle Finley's aim in life—to spend and be spent for the good of mankind—as his own. Uncle Finley did not think being a lawyer was a way of helping mankind, although Benjamin himself was not certain of this. Surely, he thought, a good lawyer does much good in the world.

On and on through the deepening twilight he rode, until his little mare drooped with weariness. All at once Benjamin too, felt tired, worn out in mind and body in a way he had never known before. Soon, he knew, he would be passing the

Red Lion Inn. Perhaps it would be best to stop there for the night.

Before he dropped off to sleep, Benjamin did as Uncle Finley had asked him to. "Dear Father in Heaven," he prayed with a fervent heart, "guide me to the path thee wishes me to follow."

The next morning when the sun streamed in through the curtainless windows, Benjamin awoke with a sense of peace. Somehow—he couldn't say why exactly—he knew now what he must do. He ate a quick breakfast of mush and a thick slice of ham and was off again for Philadelphia.

When he reached home, his mother met him at the door. "What is it, Benjamin?" she asked curiously. "You look so determined—and full of purpose."

"I am both those things, Mama," the boy replied, looking even more serious than usual, "and I want to talk to you. But first I must call upon Lawyer Tayloe and tell him I cannot read law with him. I have decided instead to study physic."

When Benjamin Rush decided to study medicine in 1760, he was not entering into a scientific profession as we know it today. Medicine in Europe was still full of superstitions handed down from the Middle Ages. Medicine in the American colonies was in an even worse state.

From the beginning, trained doctors in the colonies were rare. This was not surprising, for colonial America was a wild new country and had no attraction for Europe's medical talent.

Consequently the early colonists were forced to rely upon the questionable medical knowledge of their ministers and other prominent men. Often their advice was worse than that of the savage Indians about them. Governor Winthrop of Connecticut, for example, an intelligent man and a member of the Royal

Society in England, prescribed for a stomach-ache "hot buttered mustket balls to be taken on the full of the moon."

Although in Europe there were several great medical schools, medical knowledge itself had advanced little beyond the humoral physiology and pathology set forth by the Greek philosophers hundreds of years before Christ.

This humoral system taught that the body functions through four kinds of fluids—or humors, as they were then called. The four humors upon which bodily health depended were: blood, phlegm, black bile and yellow bile.

Each humor was associated with two of the four fundamental qualities: namely, heat, cold, moisture and dryness. Blood, for example, was considered moist and hot. Yellow bile, hot and dry. Bodily health was thought to result from the proper balance and counteraction of the four humors. Disease resulted from the excess or deficiency of one or another of them. If a person was sick because he had too much of a certain humor (or fluid) he could be restored to health by draining away the harmful excess fluid. The draining was done by bleeding, purging or sweating, according to which fluid needed to be removed.

If a patient was ill because he had too little of a certain humor, the doctor had to decide which humor was lacking. Then because it was widely believed that food and drugs consisted of the same elements, and possessed the same qualities as the body tissues, this fluid deficiency was made up by special drugs and diet.

When a patient needed bleeding, usually a special man, the surgeon, was called in. The surgeon, during most of the colonial period, had little social standing, either in Europe or in America. He was not like the physician who enjoyed the prestige of studying physic (the art of healing) through books and

theories. Nor was he forbidden by tradition handed down from the medieval clergy, as was the physician, "to soil his hands with blood."

Thus it was the surgeon, usually a barber by trade, who performed the menial jobs of bloodletting and bonesetting. In fact, it was not until 1745—the year Benjamin Rush was born— that English barbers and surgeons officially separated into two distinct groups. When a surgeon sailed to America, he was classed on the passenger list as a manual trades worker, along with the bricklayers and the carpenters.

Of course the existence of germs, bacteria and viruses was completely unknown. The dangers from flies and other insects and from rats and mice were as yet unthought of. And the perils from the lack of even the simplest sanitation seemed to worry no one. Occasionally a doctor blamed filth for disease, but he assumed the sickness came from the deadly miasmas (vapors) which floated off the filth rather than from the deadly microscopic life within.

Although William Harvey had lectured on his discovery of the circulation of the blood in 1616, just what purpose the blood served, or even how much blood the body contained, was a mystery to the learned physicians of the time.

Similarly, the structure and functions of most of the internal organs of the body were largely a matter of guesswork. Lavoisier did not discover the body's need of oxygen until 1774. Laënnec did not invent the stethoscope until 1816, and of course the microscope was still a toy. Even the presence of fever was unrecognized unless it was severe, because the clinical thermometer was not used in medicine until 1868.

But Benjamin Rush had no idea that he was sailing into falsely charted seas when he asked Dr. John Redman, Philadelphia's leading physician, to accept him as an apprentice.

Now as he waited for Dr. Redman in the latter's office, his heart bumped uncomfortably. The crackling flames from the hickory logs in the fireplace made him too warm. He walked across the room and looked with approval at the important-looking tomes in the walnut case—at the volumes by Sydenham and by Boerhaave which were fortunately written in English, and at another by Hippocrates in Greek.

Since there was no medical school or library in all the American colonies, Benjamin knew he was fortunate in finding a master who possessed this small collection of medical books. Most American doctors had no such volumes, nor had they read any. They had simply picked up their medical knowledge by watching and listening to their master as he treated his patients. Sometimes they hadn't even spent much time watching and listening, because they had also served as stable boy and personal servant all the while they were supposed to be learning their profession.

In many cases the original masters were really not doctors at all. They were simply ship's surgeons who had walked off the ship with a small supply of medicines and set up shop. Or worse yet, many so-called physicians did not have even the knowledge of the lowly surgeon. They were merely men who found it easy to make a living in a new country by proclaiming themselves doctors.

Dr. Redman, however, was no such fraud. He had been graduated from the University of Leyden in Holland where he had studied with associates of the great Boerhaave himself. He was also consulting physician to the Pennsylvania Hospital which Benjamin Franklin had helped establish in 1752 to care for sick people unable to pay for treatment.

When Dr. Redman made his rounds at the hospital, his apprentices went with him, observing all kinds of sickness and their treatment. Dr. Redman was also able to serve as a surgeon should amputation of an arm or leg be necessary. Without a doubt, Benjamin realized, Redman's apprentices would be among the best-trained young doctors in the colonies. And such training was well worth the rather large fee the doctor charged his pupils.

A sharp pounding from the next room drew the boy's attention. This noise must be coming from Dr. Redman's apothecary shop he decided. Probably the doctor's other apprentice, Sammy Treat, was pounding herbs into a powder. Preparing the drugs was, he knew, one of the chief duties of the advanced apprentice, and selling them, one of the main ways a doctor made his living. The drugs themselves were considered precious because they had to be brought over from Europe.

Benjamin's thoughts were interrupted by the ring of horse's hoofs and the grind of wheels upon the cobblestones. Through the falling snow he saw a man jump down from a small two-wheeled chair and beckon to the stable boy. Benjamin felt a prick of nervousness. The man he hoped would be his future master was home.

A moment later Dr. Redman pushed open the door to his study and stepped in, bringing with him the fresh, damp smell of snow. He was a short, stocky man of thirty-eight with searching but warm dark eyes. Benjamin saw that he was tired.

"Ah, good evening, lad. 'Tis bitter out," the doctor said with a quick look of appraisal. He tossed a worn leather case upon the couch and sank into a chair. The case fell open, and Ben saw that the two enormous knives inside were bloodstained. An unpleasant odor arose from them. He felt slightly sick.

"Eh, lad," Dr. Redman said sharply as he noticed Ben's indrawn nostrils. "I thought you wanted to become a physician."

"Indeed I do, sir." Ben averted his eyes from the vicious-looking knives. "I—I hope I may make a good one."

"Well, then, we can't have any milksop notions about a little blood or amputations or such. Matter of fact, 'tis best for a doctor not to be too sensitive to the pain of others. Not much can be done on that score, and the less the doctor suffers with his patients, the steadier his hand will be. Now, let me see, you are how old?"

"Fifteen, sir."

"A good age for an apprentice," approved Dr. Redman. "And your solemn manner is also fitting. I perceive you've been graduated from the College of New Jersey with a splendid record. But you look thin. How is your health?"

Ben hesitated. He wished he could say, "Robust, sir," but he knew he couldn't. There was that heavy cough he had to fight so often. "Fair enough, sir," he answered briskly. "Except that I seem to have a slight delicacy in my chest."

"Humph," Dr. Redman studied Ben intently. "Come here and open your shirt."

The doctor placed his ear against Ben's chest and listened for a moment. "Well, doesn't sound like a consumption. You'll grow out of it, I expect. But keep that chest protected, and try honey and linseed oil if you cough. You can move in here tomorrow—in the back room over the surgery, with Sammy Treat." The doctor stood up and bowed a dismissal.

Ben returned the bow and hurried out into the cold to run home and tell his mother the good news.

When he reached his house he found her sitting in the firelit common room reading a letter.

" 'Tis from your Uncle Finley," she said, looking up with bright eyes. "The Reverend Davies has perished from lung fever, and your uncle has just been elected the new president of the College of New Jersey."

"Uncle Finley, President," exclaimed Benjamin looking pleased. " 'Tis surely significant to hear such news the day I become apprentice to Dr. Redman."

CHAPTER FOUR

The Medical Apprentice

A year later on a raw cloudy day in February, 1762, Benjamin Rush walked slowly along Pine Street toward the small brick house of the widow Entwhistle. Mrs. Entwhistle's daughter Polly, sixteen years old like Benjamin himself, was desperately ill of a consumption. She was so ill that Dr. Redman had told Ben privately that he held no hope for her.

Because of this sad situation Benjamin dreaded visiting the girl. But Dr. Redman was laid up with a pleurisy and Sammy Treat was miles out in the country treating a farmer who had been trampled by an ox, so Ben knew he had to go.

After a year as a medical apprentice, Ben still suffered along with his patients. If he had to help with an amputation or cutting for a bladder stone, he felt helpless and shaky. But in other ways he was beginning to believe that perhaps Uncle Finley had been right in urging him to study physic. Whenever he was able to comfort or help a sick person, he felt a real glow of satisfaction. And only last week Dr. Redman had told him that Mr. Hale, the chandler, had remarked upon his sensible judgment. Thinking of this, Ben tried harder than usual to look assured as he tapped at Widow Entwhistle's door.

Mrs. Entwhistle let him in quietly. "Polly's dropped off for a nap," she whispered, "and Mrs. Gampey's resting, too." Mrs. Gampey was Polly's nurse. At the moment she lay sound asleep in bed beside the feverish girl. This fact didn't bother Benja-

min because at the time nurses often slept in the same bed
with their patients. No one knew that a consumption, or
tuberculosis as it was later called, was contagious.

"Don't waken them," the young apprentice murmured. "I'll
stop by later and see to Polly. The rest will do her good."

He left the Entwhistle home and walked several squares to
Spruce Street to call on old Mr. Beedle, the saddler. Mr.
Beedle said he felt sick all over and had a scandalous headache.
Ben set his tiny pulse glass on the table and counted the patient's pulse. When the sand had trickled through to the lower
glass, he announced, "Your pulse is full and tense, sir. You
want bleeding badly."

Then he skillfully inserted his lancet into a vein in Mr.
Beedle's arm and caught the flowing blood in a small pewter
bowl. When the bowl was full, Ben held the wound until the
blood stopped flowing. He flashed a confident smile at his
patient, "I'm sure you will remain in good humor now, Mr.
Beedle."

The saddler, who was looking rather weak and pale, peered
at him curiously. "Land sakes, Mr. Rush, ye sound more like
Dr. Redman than the doctor himself. If I didn't know ye for
yer father's son, I'd say ye was at least forty years old. Ye
sound like it anyways. Always workin', ain't ye?"

"I do not mind work," Benjamin replied decisively. "In
truth, I like it."

It was a good thing, too, that he did, Ben told himself as he
walked back to his master's apothecary shop to pound the
powders and roll the pills for the doctor's patients. If he didn't,
he never would be able to keep up with his duties as apprentice.
During the past year, he recalled, he had not had one single
day or night off. But he had learned much about the practice of
medicine.

From the beginning he had accompanied Dr. Redman on his house calls and hospital visits. He had studied the doctor's prized medical volumes, and he had copied into his Commonplace Book information which he gained from his master's exchanges of letters with other physicians.

Although Ben did not serve as Dr. Redman's personal servant, he did on occasion have to act as a nurse to patient's needing such care. He also had charge of his master's accounts. Often, when the patients could not pay in money, they settled their bill by bringing flour or potatoes, or they mended shoes or performed other services, so that bookkeeping was difficult.

Dr. Redman appreciated Ben's ability. After one year he placed him in full charge of many patients. It gave the boy a queer feeling to be responsible for the health—even for the lives—of other people. Sometimes as he watched youths his own age frolicking in the snow or boating on the river or just laughing with the girls, he wondered how it would feel to be so carefree.

During 1762 a strange killing disease appeared in a number of homes along the waterfront. Dr. Redman said he had not seen this sickness in all his years of practice, but he remembered hearing about such a disease attacking Philadelphia every thirty years or so. Just what the sickness was or how it started, no one knew.

Young Rush was horrified at the way the victims swiftly died, their faces usually a ghastly yellow. He did as Dr. Redman ordered and used mild purges and bleeding, and also tried wine and Jesuit bark, but the patients rarely recovered. Sadly, Ben entered careful notes about each case into his Commonplace Book. Thirty-one years later, when this mysterious disease struck again with far deadlier force, these notes which Ben had made as an apprentice were found to be the best record in existence of this earlier epidemic.

One day during this same year Dr. Redman showed Ben a notice in the Pennsylvania *Gazette* stating that Dr. William Shippen, Jr. was offering a course in anatomy, to be given at the State House. The course was open to medical students "and for the entertainment of any gentleman who may have the curiosity to understand the Anatomy of the Human Frame." A discussion of all necessary operations in surgery and a course in bandaging was also promised.

Benjamin reread the advertisement with mounting interest. He knew of Dr. Billy Shippen, although as a member of the wealthy and aristocratic Shippen family, Billy moved in considerably higher social circles than he did.

"The course certainly sounds interesting, sir," he said, handing the *Gazette* back to Dr. Redman.

"More than interesting," the older man shot back. " 'Tis an opportunity you should not miss. Young Shippen is reported to be an excellent male midwife and anatomist. But then," Dr. Redman tapped the ashes from his pipe into the fireplace, "he ought to be. He has had the best training available to any colonial American. Think of it, Ben. First, Billy serves as apprentice to his father who, as you know, is a splendid physician himself. Then he goes to London and studies anatomy with the famous Hunter brothers. After that he gets his degree of Doctor of Medicine from the University of Edinburgh. You could not ask for a more highly qualified man to teach anatomy, could you?"

"Indeed, I could not, sir."

Ben was aware that he himself was not learning anatomy, although this was not his master's fault. Even though Dr. Redman frequently acted as surgeon, operations in those days were mostly limited to the limbs of the body or to "cutting into the bladder for the stone." Practically no one dared cut into the abdomen or chest of a living person. They knew if they did, even if the patient survived the shock of the unbearable pain, death was almost sure to follow from infection.

Thus few doctors in America in 1760 had actually seen the inner workings of the human body. Of course, through war wounds or accidents, every doctor had at some time looked into a part of the body's interior, but none knew how the body worked as a whole.

The idea that a doctor or medical student might dissect a human body for study was regarded with horror by most Americans. They felt it was a sacrilege to treat a human body in this fashion. If a medical man wanted to know how the body was put together and how it functioned, let him, they declared, study the bodies of animals.

In London, on the other hand, the Hunter brothers instructed their anatomy students by the actual dissection of human bodies. It is true that even there corpses were hard to get since they were supposed to be only the bodies of criminals executed by the government and had to be especially petitioned for. Occasionally though, the bodies in the laboratory were of unknown persons, a fact which gave rise to many frightening stories.

But now, right here in Philadelphia, for the first time in America, a course in human anatomy was being offered. As Dr. Redman had said, it was too good an opportunity to miss. The next morning Ben went down to the State House and signed up for Dr. Shippen's lectures. Ten other medical apprentices and several full-fledged doctors signed up with him.

When Billy Shippen began his lectures, he used drawings and plaster casts to demonstrate the structure and functions of the body. This was out of deference to American feelings. But after three sessions, it was clear to both teacher and student that drawings and casts, no matter how skillfully made, could not really show how the body was put together and how it operated.

"By some means," Shippen announced to the class, "we must secure a corpse to dissect." The students looked at one another and gasped.

After two weeks' effort, Dr. Shippen succeeded in locating an unclaimed body—apparently that of a runaway slave who had died in jail. Understandably, the colonial officials wouldn't let him use the State House for dissection purposes, so Shippen took over a small building behind his father's brick mansion as a laboratory.

Here the class gathered in, as Benjamin observed, "an unease of expectancy." On a table in the center of the room lay the corpse, covered with a sheet. Without a word, Dr. Shippen beckoned the students to approach. Then he threw back the sheet and lifted the corpse's arm. He had just begun to explain what he proposed to demonstrate when from outside came furious shouts of "Murderer! Grave robber!"

Professor and students rushed to the window. They saw a crowd of angry men storming toward them from the alley. Some brandished flaming torches; others carried stones which an instant later crashed through the window. One of them hit the student next to Benjamin, and he fell to the floor, his head bleeding.

Inside the laboratory panic broke loose. The full-fledged doctors were afraid to be caught in what they considered incriminating circumstances. One hid in the chimney and another climbed into a bean barrel.

"I was afraid of this," Dr. Shippen muttered. "Stand guard

at the windows, men. Don't let the poltroons in. I'll try to talk some sense into them."

He dashed outside, raised his arms and pleaded for silence. His words were lost in a blast of catcalls and curses. "Burn the body snatchers out," one rough yelled, tossing his flaming torch at the building's roof. "Aye," shouted another, aiming a torch at Shippen himself.

Fortunately, a moment later the older Dr. Shippen with several police officers hurried to the scene, and the mob scattered.

After that, the anatomy lectures were held in an atmosphere of such tension that Benjamin could not give full attention to the demonstrations. Again and again, furious crowds gathered outside and shook the doors and windows of the laboratory. Ben admired Dr. Shippen's courage in continuing with the course, but he decided that if he really hoped to learn anatomy, he would have to study it in Europe. He didn't know when or how, but for the time being he'd concentrate on his work with Dr. Redman.

Three years later in 1765 another young American doctor, John Morgan, came home to Philadelphia from Edinburgh and also set up special courses for medical students. He presented his courses differently from the way Billy Shippen did, and because of this the seeds of a bitter hatred were sown between the two men.

The trouble probably began in Edinburgh where John Morgan, like Billy Shippen, was studying for an advanced degree in medicine. Morgan, like Shippen, was a member of a rich and aristocratic Philadelphia family. He had been Dr. Redman's apprentice for over five years. Then he had served as a lieutenant and surgeon with the provincial troops in the French and Indian War.

After his military service Morgan had gone to London to study anatomy with the Hunter brothers and then on to the University of Edinburgh where he was considered one of the most brilliant students ever enrolled there.

When Morgan came to the Scottish university, Shippen was almost finished with his studies and ready to go home. Naturally the two Philadelphians spent much time together. Neither thought the colonial system of studying medicine was much good. Shippen's idea was to improve the apprenticeship system by offering more lectures on many subjects, including anatomy and obstetrics. He urged Dr. Morgan to join him by giving lectures to the apprentices on the theory of physic.

John Morgan wasn't sure he liked the apprenticeship system at all—even with advanced lecture courses available. He told Shippen he wanted to think about the matter more carefully.

After Dr. Shippen had sailed back to Philadelphia, however, Dr. Morgan definitely decided that Shippen's idea for reforming American medicine was not broad enough. Colonial practice, he believed, needed to be made over completely. It was not enough for two physicians, however well qualified themselves, to give private lessons to any apprentice who signed up for a course.

Dr. Morgan thought that in order to get rid of long-standing abuses in the colonies, a real medical university was necessary— one which could offer training in all branches of medical science. This medical university, in his opinion, should not take apprentices merely because they could pay the fees, but rather because they could meet stiff entrance requirements. Then when this university gave a degree of Doctor of Medicine, the degree would have real value.

Morgan's plan, of course, is the one medical students follow today, but in 1763 it was startlingly new. Because his plan was untried, Dr. Morgan sought the opinion of some of the leading

British physicians. These men encouraged the young American doctor to present his ideas to Thomas Penn, the Proprietor of Pennsylvania. Penn was so impressed that he immediately wrote the trustees of the College of Philadelphia and recommended that they authorize Dr. John Morgan to set up a medical school there. In his letter Penn suggested that they use Morgan's plan for the education of colonial medical students.

It was a seemingly innocent letter that Penn wrote the college trustees. But when Dr. Shippen heard about it, he was enraged, for the letter did not even mention his name.

At first, Dr. Morgan was the only professor in the new medical school. But three months later Dr. Billy Shippen asked the trustees if he, too, could present his lectures in anatomy and obstetrics there. At the same time he demanded that the trustees designate him—not John Morgan, as senior professor. The trustees voted otherwise, however. Then there was strange talk all over Philadelphia.

Benjamin heard, for example, that Dr. Shippen, Jr. was furious with Dr. Morgan, not only for having returned to Philadelphia in such triumph but also for having won public credit for establishing the first medical school in America. Actually, Dr. Shippen stated, the medical school was *his* idea. Dr. Morgan, he declared, had stolen it from him in Edinburgh.

When he heard these remarks, Benjamin Rush agreed with those who said that if Billy Shippen had really planned to start a medical school as part of the College of Philadelphia, he would have done so when he first came back in 1762. After all, his own father was a trustee of the college and could have helped him with the project. Why then, they asked, had Shippen set himself up as a private lecturer for three years? And then, only when Dr. Morgan presented his plan for a medical school in 1765, did he claim this had been his idea all along? There was no question in Benjamin's mind where credit for the medical school really belonged, and which man was truly interested in medical education and not in personal glory.

Benjamin's master Dr. Redman openly spoke in favor of Dr. Morgan. As soon as the new School of Medicine opened its doors in May, 1765, he urged Benjamin to enroll in Morgan's class on the theory of physic—if he could find the time.

"*If* he could find the time," Benjamin thought wryly, "that is indeed a problem."

But somehow he managed to take Dr. Morgan's course just as he managed to get through his other studies. He had been Dr. Redman's apprentice for over four years now. During that period he had not missed ten days from his duties, nor had he spent three nights away from his master's house.

As the months went by, these duties increased, for Sammy Treat had left to set up his own office, and Dr. Redman was often ill. During these times there was only nineteen-year-old Benjamin to take care of a large practice. Often when the long day was done he fell into bed with his clothes on. Then he slept heavily until daylight or until the clanging of the emergency bell in the office below brought him down the stairs at a run.

Occasionally toward evening Benjamin snatched time to have a raisin cake and a cup of coffee at the popular London Coffee House on Front and Market streets. Probably because Mr. Bradford, the proprietor, was so outspoken against the power of the British throne, the Coffee House was the gathering place for people who felt the colonies were being unfairly taxed and governed.

Lately, Benjamin noticed, the conversation at the Coffee House was mostly about the Stamp Act which the British government had passed in March. This act, by which the British hoped to collect a lot of money to help their shaky finances at home, required that special revenue stamps be bought and placed upon newspapers and other printed material. Many colonists believed it was an unfair way of taking their money, and they resented it.

All that summer of 1765—the summer that Patrick Henry in Virginia had shouted, "If this be treason, make the most of it," Benjamin Rush thought about the growing quarrels between the colonies and Britain. Many of his fellow colonists, perhaps most of those he knew, still considered themselves Englishmen. He didn't. England seemed too remote, too different from the bright, busy, energetic young country he loved. In America, he felt, almost everyone—no matter what his background—could have his say and could work to enjoy the good things of the rich country. In England, he had been told, birth and position counted for so much.

But even though he felt this way, Benjamin Rush believed in the divine right of kings. "Kings were born to rule," he remarked to his Coffee House tablemate one August afternoon. "It is the proper thing. Without them—" he paused. The next instant he jumped up to greet a tall, fashionably dressed man who had stopped at his table.

"Good day to you, Benjamin. Would you be good enough to wait upon me at my office at your earliest convenience?"

"Certainly, Dr. Morgan." Benjamin's cheeks were hot with excitement though he tried to appear calm. What could the famous Dr. Morgan want with him?

When he hurried to Dr. Morgan's office the next afternoon, the twenty-five-year-old physician came right to the point.

"Ben," he said, "Dr. Redman tells me you have about completed your apprenticeship—that he cannot teach you any more. What do you plan to do next? Set up your own establishment?"

"Why, no, sir—not yet. I do not feel my medical education is yet complete. I have a little money saved, and Dr. Redman has advised me to study further at Edinburgh."

"Ah," Dr. Morgan's fine dark eyes brightened with approval. "That is what I hoped you would do. Although you are doing well in my materia medica class, I know that our new college of medicine is not yet ready for a student as advanced as you. Among other things, we need a professor of chemistry." He paused and looked keenly at Benjamin.

Benjamin was interested in chemistry, and he read all the articles he could get which dealt with this new science. Now he gazed back at Dr. Morgan. "Indeed, sir, a professor of chemistry would be most valuable. I for one should like to know much more than I do about the subject. In fact, I plan to take Dr. Black's lectures on that subject at Edinburgh."

"Good," Morgan leaned forward and looked steadily into the young apprentice's eyes. "Ben, if you agree to specialize in that subject at Edinburgh, I will endeavor to hold open the chair of chemistry for you here at the college—until you have won your degree."

Ben blinked with pleased surprise. To be told at nineteen that he would have such a fine position as professor of chemistry waiting for him was more than he could bear. Imagine, he, Benjamin Rush a professor of chemistry! ! !

But his joy was dimmed in July of 1766, when Uncle Finley was brought to Philadelphia dying of a mysterious ailment. Dr. Redman did what he could, and toward the end, Benjamin sat with his uncle all through the dreary night hours, but it was no use. Before many days, fifty-one-year-old Samuel Finley, eminent minister, and President of the College of New Jersey, died of his baffling sickness.

Benjamin was heartsick. He had loved Uncle Finley and he was glad now that in his last hours Uncle Finley had again blessed him for taking up the study of physic.

CHAPTER FIVE

A Student at Edinburgh

In September, 1766, twenty-one-year-old Benjamin Rush sailed for Britain on the *Friendship*. With him was Jonathan Potts, another young medical student, also bound for the University of Edinburgh. The voyage was so stormy that the *Friendship* was nearly lost off the coast of Ireland and almost wrecked on the coast of Wales. Jonathan got along fine on the trip, but Benjamin was sick the whole time. He couldn't even sleep unless he drugged himself with laudanum first.

When the *Friendship* dropped anchor at Liverpool seven weeks later, Benjamin was the most thankful person on board. He and Jonathan stayed in England only long enough to pick up a letter of introduction from Benjamin Franklin, Agent of the province of Pennsylvania, to Dr. Cullen of the Edinburgh University Medical School. Visiting Franklin first was common procedure for young American colonials because this best-known and best-loved American in Europe did much to smooth the way of his countrymen who were abroad for study.

Their audience with Franklin over, the two Americans boarded the heavy coach for Edinburgh. More than a week later they arrived in the Scottish capital and were astonished by their first view of lofty Castle Rock. Atop this gigantic mass of stone their fascinated eyes rested upon ancient Edinburgh Castle. Solid and forbidding, it loomed above them, its huge gray towers fading into the mist. In the distance through the haze they could see the dull silver ribbon of the Firth of Forth.

"My boots and buskins, 'tis really impressive," commented Jonathan in an awed tone. Benjamin nodded, but actually as he gazed around at the Gothic-looking city, grimy with smoke and age, he felt depressed. Edinburgh seemed so crowded. Eighty thousand people, he had heard—twice the population of Philadelphia—were jammed into one third less space. Within the city's medieval walls, backed up against the steep hills on one side and a ravine on the other, the people had nowhere to build their houses but up—one on top of each other.

Benjamin stared at the blackish stone buildings, some towering fifteen stories above the narrow streets. How many families lived in each one, he wondered. The stairs, running straight up to the top, were really like perpendicular streets. With land so scarce, the houses had no yards. He watched a woman struggle up ten flights, carrying two caddies of water which she had drawn from a nearby well.

The next day, when he and Jonathan found satisfactory lodgings with two maiden ladies named Galloway whose home was clean and only four stories above the street, he felt happier about living in Edinburgh.

As soon as they unpacked their clothes, they went to the University to obtain tickets of admission to the lectures.

The schedule Ben selected was a rugged one, but he had grown used to hard work and long hours during his apprenticeship. Often he wished the winter daylight in Edinburgh wasn't so short. He found it trying to rise before seven and read for two hours by candlelight, then go off to Dr. Cullen's lecture on "Institutes of Medicine" (physiology). Fortunately, Dr. Cullen lectured in English instead of in Latin as the other professors did, so note-taking wasn't difficult.

At ten he gulped a breakfast of porridge and tea, and then

spent two hours carefully transcribing the notes of the lecture into a permanent notebook. This transcription was important because in those days there were few textbooks. Each student had to make his own from the professor's lectures. If a student planned to teach or practice medicine, these notes were especially valuable and had to be put into an accurate, easily read and permanent form.

From twelve until one o'clock Ben "walked the wards" of the Royal Infirmary, observing the patients and their treatment. From one until three he was in Dr. Monro's anatomy class. After that he had a quick dinner at his boardinghouse. Often the dinner made him drowsy, but he had to rush to Dr. Joseph Black's chemistry class. Next he listened to Dr. Hope's botany lectures or, on alternate days, Dr. Gregory's talks on the practice of medicine. At six he attended more anatomy demonstrations.

After seven, Ben relaxed until nine when he ate supper—a thick barley broth flecked with bits of mutton. Then he worked again on his lecture notes, and studied Latin and French. When the bells of St. Giles told him it was midnight, he put away his notes and went to bed.

Benjamin looked forward with special interest to his chemistry class. This was partly because of the position Dr. Morgan was holding open for him in Philadelphia, and partly because his professor was one of Britain's foremost chemists—Dr. Joseph Black.

One dreary November afternoon he watched Black prepare a demonstration. On the laboratory table sat two covered vessels filled with limewater. At Black's request, a student stepped up to one vessel and blew into the liquid through a glass tube. The limewater turned milky white.

Next Dr. Black poured vinegar over chalk. By using a spe-

cial apparatus he caught in a jar the colorless "air" which escaped. (Today we call this sort of "air" a gas.) This procedure
completed, he burned charcoal and once again imprisoned the
escaping air in a jar.

"Well, gentlemen," he announced, "before your eyes I have
done an unusual thing. By burning ordinary charcoal and by
pouring acid on chalk I have released the air which is com-
monly fixed in these substances."

There was a murmur of excitement among the students, most
of whom already knew of Black's fame as the discoverer of fixed
air, or carbon dioxide, as it is now called. But they soon quieted,
for the chemist was continuing with his experiment.

Benjamin leaned forward as Black said, "Now watch carefully, gentlemen." From one of the jars he directed some of the
imprisoned air into the limewater. The liquid turned a milky
white, just as it had done when the student blew into it.

Black looked at the students' fascinated faces. "There," he
said with emphasis, "is one test for fixed air—it turns limewater
milky. Here is another." He lighted a candle and plunged it
into one of the jars of fixed air. The flame went out.

There was a stir in the class. "But sir," one student called
excitedly, "did not the breathing of the student into the limewater also turn it milky?"

"Ah, you are observant," the chemist said, pleased. "It did
indeed. It would seem that all animals, human and otherwise,
exhale fixed air from their lungs. Undoubtedly this air has many
peculiar properties."

During the demonstration Benjamin had leaned so far forward his neck hurt. Now he relaxed. Fixed air! The very words
had a magic sound. This, he told himself happily, was precisely
the new chemical learning he had come to Edinburgh to find.

In truth though, neither Benjamin Rush nor any other

student of the time was learning much chemistry, as we understand the science today. For this subject, like medicine itself, was still entangled in the false, mystical beliefs of the Middle Ages. Mid-eighteenth century chemists, like the alchemists before them, believed that there were only four elements—earth, air, fire and water.

They thought that all the substances in the world were made from some mixture of these four which, since they were elements, could never be broken into parts. Moreover, they were sure that one element could be changed into another. When a chemist of Rush's time noticed the earthy residue left behind by evaporating water, he thought the water had been changed into earth. All chemists of the time believed that one metal could be changed into another—if only one could learn how.

Until Lavoisier developed his theory of combustion in 1783, no one realized that air—with its oxygen—was needed for burning. And until combustion was understood, modern chemistry could not develop.

As a good student, Benjamin Rush absorbed all these false theories and remembered them so well that in 1773, after he had been teaching chemistry for four years, he wrote to Benjamin Franklin:

> The Doctor (Joseph Black) deserves great credit for his application of fixed air to medicine. To his remarks on the subject, I would beg leave to add one more. A large quantity of fixed air is discharged in perspiration. This is proved by a candle immediately ceasing to burn if it be put under the bedclothes of a person who is well-covered in bed.

The time Benjamin spent studying chemistry at Edinburgh was not entirely wasted, however, for although Professor Black's basic reasoning was wrong, he did impart much practical knowledge to his students. Before he graduated, young Rush learned many things in the field of applied chemistry which would be useful to people who hoped to develop and build industries in their own country. He learned, for example, how to manufacture china and cotton cloth, and how to make soap—and gunpowder.

The medical school at the University of Edinburgh was famous because it combined the study of the theory of medicine with actual observation of patients in the hospital, a rare procedure in 1766. Thus an important part of Benjamin Rush's medical training in Scotland lay in "walking the wards."

Along with the other students, he went daily to the Royal Infirmary and "walked the wards" with the attending physician. He listened carefully while the doctor stood by the patient and in a loud voice questioned him about the history of his disease. As the physician spoke, two clinical clerks (especially selected senior students) took down his every word. Then in carrying tones, as though he were making a speech, the doctor gave his prescriptions and directions for the care of this particular case.

At the next visit, the clinical clerk read back all the information of the previous day. When the physician asked the patient about any new symptoms and the effect of the drugs, the clerk repeated both the doctor's questions and the patient's answers in such loud tones that all the students, even those far off in the room, could hear. Next, the physician pointed out the different methods of treatment which could be used in each case, Then he offered his opinion of how each case would end. If no cure could be expected, the doctor said so, and the clinical clerk clearly repeated this sad fact to the students, the patients and the rest of the ward.

As the clinical clerk spoke, each student took down every word of both doctor and patient in a Case Book which was to be kept and studied in later years.

Undoubtedly the learned physicians' prognosis of each case would have been more accurate if medicine itself hadn't been floundering in the cross currents of the various "systems of medicine." These systems arose as the medical schools tried frantically to fit in the new discoveries of physics and chemistry with what they already thought to be true about the human body. Trouble arose because their basic beliefs about the body, according to the old humoral theory, were wrong, but they still did not have enough accurate new knowledge of physics and chemistry to put them on the right track.

Consequently all the new systems were partly right but mostly wrong, and the followers of each were often violent in their beliefs. Sometimes they fought with fists and even with swords to defend their theories.

Of course the day was coming when actual laboratory tests would show what definitely did go on in the body, but when Benjamin was at Edinburgh no professor knew enough about the true workings of the human system to give the student a sound basis upon which to work.

Unfortunately, one of the most inaccurate of the theorizers was the celebrated Dr. Cullen himself. Roughly, Cullen believed that disease was due either to a too-strong or to a too-weak excitement of the nervous system. "Treatment must aim," he declared, "either to build up nervous energy by restorative drugs, drinks and high diet, or to reduce it by bleedings, purgings and low diet."

As he listened to Dr. Cullen's charming and persuasive lectures, Benjamin, like the other students, was completely won over to his theories.

"When I get back to Philadelphia," he promised himself, "I will pass on Dr. Cullen's great knowledge to the uninformed, old-fashioned doctors there. It dismays me to think that most of them still practice by the ancient humoral method."

Although his studies left little time for outside activities, Benjamin was friendly with the twenty other Americans at the school. Of these, perhaps the most outstanding was twenty-five-year-old Adam Kuhn.

Kuhn was a Pennsylvania German who had already studied botany in Sweden with Linnaeus. Now he was only one year short of getting his medical degree at Edinburgh. All the professors were impressed with his knowledge and thoroughness. Dr. Cullen even declared that he knew no one in the world better qualified to teach botany and materia medica than this big, slow-spoken colonial.

Benjamin used to watch Kuhn as he walked methodically through the Royal Infirmary Gardens, lovingly inspecting each herb. In those days herbs were made into valuable medicines, and most hospitals not only raised their own vegetables but many of their drugs as well.

Benjamin tried to be friendly with Kuhn, but the latter was so stiff and formal that he soon gave up trying. Still, he wrote Dr. Morgan that Kuhn would make a fine professor of botany for the new medical school.

It was not an American student, however, but a Scottish one named John Bostock who had the greatest influence on Benjamin's life. Twenty-seven-year-old Bostock had a mind as sharp as a rapier and a wit to match. It was his nature to accept no theory, no philosophy, without questioning it.

Benjamin had first been attracted to him when he learned that Bostock's great-grandfather, like his own, had commanded a troop of horse under Oliver Cromwell. For the same reason Bostock was interested in the American. "We are both," he declared, "descended from freedom-loving stock, and we should never forget it."

The two young men fell into the habit of walking through the hilly streets and talking politics. "So you are a republican, Rush," Bostock said abruptly one day.

"I—a republican?" Ben echoed in a startled tone. "I—I don't know, Bostock. I don't know as I'd go *that* far."

"You tell me that you denounced the Stamp Act," Bostock persisted. "You did not think the King had the right to tax you without your consent, did you? I am sure there are many things the King does that you do not believe he has a right to do. And you are quite correct, Rush. Why should the King have such authority over you or me or any man? Think about it now. Why should he? When you come down to it, we really do not need kings—do we?"

For a long moment Benjamin didn't answer. Inwardly he was shocked by his friend's statement. "I do not know what to say, John," he replied slowly. "All my life I have been taught to consider kings as essential to the political order as the sun is to the order of our solar system."

John Bostock barely hid his scorn. "Poppycock! Undoubtedly that is what the agents of royalty have taught you, Ben. But now, think and read for yourself. After all, you are twenty-one years old."

That was the beginning of it. "From that day," Benjamin Rush wrote later, "all my reading, observations, and reflexions tended more and more to show the absurdity of hereditary power, and to prove that no form of government can be rational but that which is derived from the sufferages of the people who

are the subjects of it. This great and active truth became a ferment in my mind."

And so, although he did not suspect it at the time, these
political talks Benjamin Rush had with a Scottish student had
as much effect upon his life and medical career as anything he
learned at the University of Edinburgh.

CHAPTER SIX

The First Hard Years

In June, 1768, Benjamin Rush received the coveted degree of Doctor of Medicine from the University of Edinburgh. His first thought now was to sail home, but he didn't feel that he had yet learned all he could and should in Europe. In September he left for London to study with Dr. William Hunter and to "walk the hospitals" there.

At that time perhaps the greatest hospital in London was St. Thomas, founded in 1552 by Edward VI. Benjamin felt fortunate to be allowed to "walk the wards" at this ancient institution where he could observe the practice of the most noted English doctors. The hospital itself, however, did not please him. The odors were dreadful, so bad in fact that whenever the governors of the hospital were to meet, the maids spent hours beforehand "strowing sweet herbs and flowers in the hall and staircase."

At night the wards were unspeakably dreary, frightening even, with the moans of the patients rising from the gloom. The place was lit only by an occasional candle, made in the hospital kitchen from left-over mutton fat. It was difficult to see which patient needed attention.

Some of the doctors too appeared not to have their patients' interest at heart. Dr. Mark Akenside, Principal Physician at St. Thomas and Doctor to the Queen, was openly rough and cruel to the poor patients. As he made his rounds, wearing an enormous white wig and an extra-long sword, neither he nor his gentlemen apprentices would dream of soiling their hands by touching the sick. In fact to be certain the hospital dirt wouldn't touch him, Dr. Akenside was always preceded by two men with brooms who swept a path for him.

There were, of course, some fine doctors, notably Sir John Pringle, the founder of modern military medicine. Dr. Pringle was so impressed with the young American doctor's ability that he invited him to join a medical club which met and debated at his home.

Benjamin was also asked to the homes of other celebrated men. The famous Quaker physician John Fotheringill often had him to breakfast. So did George Whitefield, one of the most eloquent preachers of modern times. On occasion the young doctor dined with Dr. Samuel Johnson, Oliver Gold-smith and Sir Joshua Reynolds, the artist. He spent many agree-able evenings with another noted Pennsylvanian, the painter Benjamin West—later President of the Royal Academy of Art. And for a time he lived with Benjamin Franklin and accom-panied him to court.

All during these six exciting months in London, Benjamin absorbed the talk and ideas of the highly creative, cultured and important people about him. But still he wasn't satisfied. Per-haps, he thought, I should travel to the Continent and see what else I can learn about medicine.

In February he departed for Paris. Before he left, Benjamin Franklin gave him letters of introduction to several French scientists and philosophers. As in London, Ben visited many of the outstanding thinkers of the nation. He was surprised how often their conversation dealt with the American colonies and their growing quarrels with England.

But even though he admired the French scientists, their

hospitals shocked him. They were, he decided, even more backward than those in London. The great and ancient Hôtel Dieu, of which he had heard so much, was one of the worst. It was offensive and crowded. Sometimes four patients lay in one bed. Since the other hospitals seemed equally bad, he had he concluded nothing to gain by staying longer in France. Besides, his money was nearly gone. At the end of five weeks, he packed his bags and his ever-present notebooks and started back for London—and *home*.

The dawn of July 16, 1769, found Benjamin Rush sitting on the deck of a homeward-bound ship. He was studying a Bible, written in German, which he had borrowed from a steerage passenger. Suddenly he heard the lookout cry "Land."

"Land!" He rushed to the rail. There it was—the beloved country he had not seen for three years. His eyes misted as he "viewed the American shore with a rapture that near set his heart to bursting."

Four days later in Philadelphia he bounded from the stage-coach and ran to his mother and sister Rebecca. Behind him, Jacob, who had ridden to Bristol on horseback to meet him, struggled with the luggage and a box of precious chemical apparatus.

"Benjamin, Benjamin," his mother sobbed happily, holding out her arms. Rebecca, too, was crying with joy. It was more than the sensitive young doctor could stand. Tears ran down his dusty face. An instant later, however, he smiled and said, "Now stop this, Mama. You, too, Rebecca. I am home—and I plan never to leave this blessed land again."

"Praise Heaven for that," his mother said, then added, "My, you look splendid, son. You are taller, and more slender, are you not?"

"And how much in fashion," added Rebecca admiringly. "Wherever in Philadelphia could one find such an elegant tailor?"

"Oh, nonsense, Sister," Ben laughed, rubbing her cheek. "I am still the same plain me."

But he wasn't really. He admitted that to himself the next day as he stood before a looking glass in his mother's entry hall plaiting his light-brown hair into a small queue.

After all, he reflected, there was no denying that he had spent the past three years associating with some of the greatest minds and most prominent men in Britain. He couldn't help but know that at twenty-three he had seen more of the world than had most people in the colonies, and that he definitely was one of the best-educated men on this side of the Atlantic.

If Benjamin Rush remembered a story Uncle Finley had once told about a pupil named Cecil Know-It-All, he gave no indication of it as he completed his coiffure and went to look at a small house in Arch Street he had heard was for hire.

It wasn't long, however, before he realized that even with all his superior training, making his living in Philadelphia wasn't going to be easy. Like any other young doctor, he would have to build his practice patient by patient. And *paying* patients weren't abundant.

For one thing, people in those days didn't call a physician until they had tried all the home remedies first. If these failed, or the patient was so sick he was afraid of dying, or surgery was needed, or a childbirth was too difficult for a midwife's skill, then they sent for a doctor.

Benjamin found also that the already established physicians guarded their practices with a jealousy which often stooped to low levels of backbiting and malice. As a matter of fact, in the colonies unless a young doctor belonged to a powerful family or enjoyed the patronage of some great man or a special religious sect, there was only one way for him to begin his practice. He had to work among the poor. This, however, was all right with Benjamin, for years ago he had been impressed with Dr. Boerhaave's remark, "The poor are my best patients, for God is their paymaster."

The poor themselves were grateful. When he healed them of their sickness, they were quick to spread the word that he was a good doctor. But he had to eat and pay his part of the rent for the little house on Arch Street which he now shared with Jacob and his sister Rebecca. Like Benjamin, Jacob and Rebecca were having a hard time financially. Jacob, who had just been admitted to the bar, was saving money to pay for further study at the Middle Temple in London. Rebecca had been deserted by her husband.

It was lucky for Benjamin that he had the chemistry professorship at the College of Philadelphia. Although it didn't pay much, the income was certain, and naturally the position gave him some prestige.

At twenty-three, Benjamin Rush—the first formal professor of chemistry in America—was the youngest member of the faculty, although they were mostly young. Dr. Morgan, Professor of Theory and Practice of Medicine was thirty-four; Dr. Shippen, Jr., Professor of Anatomy, Surgery and Midwifery was thirty-three; Dr. Adam Kuhn, Professor of Botany and Materia Medica, twenty-eight, and Dr. Thomas Bond, fifty-nine. All had received their doctor's degree from the University of Edinburgh and as a reminder of their debt to the Scottish institution, they had a stone thistle emblazoned above the doorway of the first medical college in America.

On the first day of class, Benjamin stood before the dozen young men who had enrolled, and nervously set up the apparatus for a demonstration on salts and alkalies. He was nervous because the chemical apparatus, the gift of the proprietor of the province himself, was the most elaborate in the colonies and would be difficult to replace.

When every gleaming piece of glass and tubing were ready, Benjamin looked seriously at his students and said, "Gentlemen, this chemical knowledge you are about to learn will be of the greatest utility. You know there are in our country countless springs and minerals and earths to be discovered and put to use in a thousand ways yet unknown.

"This morning we will discuss how potash may be made. You know that this substance will be most useful, particularly to people settling our endless western forests—especially as it is a product that can be made quickly and sold for cash."

This was the first of a series of practical lectures on a variety of subjects—the chemistry of glass and china making, the use of vegetable acids in food preservation, and the manufacture of gunpowder.

For the first year of his teaching, Benjamin used the notes he had taken in Dr. Black's course at Edinburgh. But then he decided his students might understand the subject better if they had a simple little textbook to follow. So in 1770 he wrote and published the first chemistry textbook in America. It was called *A Syllabus of a Course of Lectures in Chemistry*, and it was used for many years, chiefly because its chemical tables of various medical preparations proved so useful to doctors.

None of the professors at the medical college made their living solely by teaching. They all had private medical practices, and to these they devoted most of their attention. Benjamin often saw the prosperous ones, Drs. Morgan, Shippen and Bond, driving over the cobblestones as they made their calls in their chairs. Sometimes Dr. Kuhn, clattering by on horseback, gave him a stiff nod. But Benjamin himself went from patient to patient on foot, even though many of them lived as far away as Southwark and the Northern Liberties.

It would be a long time, he feared, before he could afford any other means of transportation. True, after only six months of practice, he had as many patients as he could handle, but few were able to pay for their care. Just this morning he had made sixteen calls and had charged for only one of them. To make matters more unprofitable, when these poor patients were unable to buy necessary medicines, Benjamin supplied the drugs free from his own store of supplies.

One thing, however, did bring him some paying patients. This was the great dread the colonists had of smallpox. Possibly this disease wasn't as feared in America as it was in London, where it had at times killed nearly half the population. But it still struck terror to all who had not already had it.

Today, as a preventative, we use vaccination—discovered by Jenner in 1798. Vaccination is safe because the serum is made from a mild disease appearing in cows, called cowpox. But in 1769 when Benjamin set up his practice, the only known guard against smallpox was inoculation—a dangerous method because it used the deadly smallpox virus itself.

In London, Benjamin had spent hours at the Inoculating Hospital learning Dr. Sutton's newer method. With this, serum from the smallpox blister in its early stages was injected into a small puncture in the arm. Earlier inoculators had put pus from the smallpox pustule—a later stage—into a long gash in the arm, and often secondary infections resulted. Sometimes severe cases of smallpox itself developed. The Suttonian method, however, brought on lighter, seldom fatal, cases.

As soon as word got around that young Dr. Rush was using

this safer way of fighting smallpox, many patients hurried to
him.

Naturally, some of these inoculation patients later consulted
him for other troubles. But even so, it was hard going. Benjamin
himself described it this way.

> From the time of my settlement in Philadelphia in 1769
> 'till 1775, I led a life of constant labor and self-denial. My
> shop was crowded with the poor in the morning and at
> meal times, and nearly every street and alley in the city
> was visited by me every day.
>
> There are few old huts now standing in the ancient
> parts of the city in which I have not attended sick people.
> Often have I ascended the upper story of these huts by a
> ladder, and many hundred times have been obliged to rest
> my weary limbs upon the bedside of the sick (from want
> of chairs) where I was sure I risqued not only taking their
> disease but being infected by vermin. More than once did
> I suffer from the latter.
>
> Nor did I hasten from these abodes of poverty and mis-
> ery. Where no help was available, I have often remained
> in them long eno' to administer my prescriptions, particu-
> larly bleeding and glysters (enemas) with my own hands.
> . . . I review these scenes with heartfelt pleasure. . . .
> To His goodness in accepting my services to His poor chil-
> dren I ascribe the innumerable blessings of my life.

While Benjamin spent his days with his patients and students, his nights were devoted to study. He seldom went to
bed before midnight. Many a time he heard the watchman cry
"three o'clock" before he put out his candle. Often he was so
tired he could scarcely stay awake. Then, if it was winter he
would excite his mind by increasing the heat and blaze of the

fire. If it was summer, he would step out on his balcony and breathe deeply of the fresh air rolling in from the river.

Philadelphians watched this new young doctor with interest as he stepped briskly through the narrow cobblestoned streets. He was always dressed immaculately in a drab, gray-green suit and well-polished black shoes with silver buckles. In one hand he carried his cylinder-shaped drug and instrument case, and in the other he swung a fine, gold-headed cane—the mark of a trained physician. His eyes were keen and strikingly blue, his complexion clear and fresh. On his face they noted a grave, wise look, quite suitable to his calling.

Sometimes they wondered why many of the older doctors treated him with noticeable unfriendliness. Benjamin wondered, too. After all, was he not giving these older doctors the benefit of the latest medical discoveries he himself had acquired with much study and expense at Edinburgh? To some of them he said, "It is regrettable that you still try to cure your patients by Boerhaave's outdated humoral theories. Why don't you try Cullen's modern methods? I am sure you will cure many more patients if you do?" Benjamin meant well, but his self-assurance and youth made him seem lacking in tact.

Not only was twenty-three-year-old Benjamin Rush eager to explain Cullen's theories to any doctor who would listen, but he followed the custom of the day and published his thoughts in the newspapers. His essays were well written, but his talents appeared wasted as far as his colleagues were concerned. Their only reaction was annoyance.

Some of these doctors were also old hands at publishing their ideas in the newspapers. Soon angry slurs and ridicule were directed publicly both at the new medical system and at its zealous disciple young Dr. Rush. Benjamin clamped his lips tight and grew more positive and tactless than ever.

One day his mother worriedly remarked, "Son, you will not give an inch to gain a foot, will you?" In reply Benjamin's voice became clipped and emphatic. "Right is right, Mama," he said. "Facts are the moralities of medicine. They never change."

Dr. Rush did not confine his opinions to medical matters. He also spoke frequently against slavery, a practice he abhorred to his soul. To further fight this evil, he wrote a pamphlet on the subject—one of the first in America. The pamphlet angered a number of wealthy, slave-owning Philadelphians. "Let Dr. Rush stick to his physic," they muttered ominously, "and not meddle with controversy foreign to his business."

Jacob Rush heard of these remarks before Benjamin did. He reported them immediately to his brother who was in his "shop" pounding herbs into a powder. "You make enemies by the score," he warned. "You had best be more discreet."

"Yes, I know, Jacob," Benjamin angrily banged the pestle against the mortar. "An indiscreet zeal for truth, justice or humanity has cost more to the persons who exercised it than the total want of zeal for anything good. But threats will not stay my pen."

During these years from 1769 to 1775 Benjamin, in addition to angering the older doctors and the slaveholders, was also busily stepping on the sensitive political toes of many rich and powerful Philadelphians who believed in being entirely loyal to the English king.

His talks with the radical John Bostock in Edinburgh were still, as he said, "a ferment in his mind." With every passing day he felt more strongly that the King had no right to rule the colonies as he often did—without the consent of the governed.

When he could snatch a few minutes from his duties, he liked to sit in the City Tavern with friends—mostly young

Scottish merchants of the neighborhood—and discuss the political situation as he saw it. Since he made no effort to keep his voice low, before long everyone in Philadelphia knew exactly where Dr. Benjamin Rush stood on the management of colonial affairs.

"Rush is a rebel," muttered some. "He should be driven out of town."

"Rush is a patriot," declared others, and thought how they might use this fiery physician in the fight for freedom.

CHAPTER SEVEN

The Doctor Helps Write
A Famous Pamphlet

But even as Dr. Rush debated with his companions in City Tavern, trouble deepened between the American colonies and Britain. Most colonists favored working out some agreement with the mother country over the various disputes, such as taxation. A number of more radical thinkers, however, like John Adams, his cousin Samuel Adams, and Patrick Henry were considering outright independence. Benjamin Rush was among these radicals.

In September, 1774, when the first Continental Congress met in Philadelphia, Benjamin, as one of the committee elected for the purpose, rode part away along the road to greet the New England delegates. At Frankford he was asked to sit in the same carriage with stocky John Adams who plied him with questions.

"Tell me," Adams asked, "how do Philadelphians really feel about the British government? And what about the character and personality of some of the leaders? I hear they are strong in the anti-British movement, but since I have met only a few, I cannot be sure. Do you really think," he asked Benjamin in low tones, "they can be trusted as patriots?"

Dr. Rush was proud of his role as "interpreter" of the Philadelphia scene to the delegates, most of whom he grew to know rather well. John and Samuel Adams stayed at his house; many of the others were guests for dinner. A few such as Patrick Henry even talked politics while Benjamin inoculated them against smallpox.

As the days went by, the twenty-nine-year-old doctor found it hard to stick to his medical duties. Talks among the delegates went on continually all over the city—in Carpenter's Hall, at the taverns and at private dinners. Sometimes when the doctor himself spoke out frankly for independence, his feelings were so strong that the color flamed high in his cheeks.

The First Continental Congress ended, however, with nothing much being done. Before the delegates left, they decided once more merely to ask George III and his ministers to play fair with their American colonies.

The fact that the delegates had gone home did not mean that the tension between the colonies and Britain was lessening. Rather, thought Benjamin uneasily, it was increasing. Soon there might be actual fighting. Then, he wondered, what would happen? He was concerned about the great division of thought among the Americans. In his opinion, not enough of them saw the need for complete independence. All they asked from the mother country was better treatment as Englishmen—the same treatment, they said, that Englishmen in England received from their rulers.

If only, the doctor thought, there was a way to make the colonists realize that their country's future lay in complete separation from Britain. If only they could read something which would explain the situation simply and forcefully— With this in mind, he began to gather material for a propaganda pamphlet on the necessity for American independence.

Every time a thought on the subject struck him, he put it down in his Commonplace Book. Little by little the material

grew until there was a notebook full. "Soon, I'll write the independence pamphlet," he promised himself. "Soon. The times
cry out for such a treatise."

One sunshiny day in February, 1775, he decided he was
entitled to a few hours' holiday. He hastened to Robert Aitkin's
bookstore on Letitia Court, which had more fine books in it
than any other shop in the province. And in addition, the store
was the home of that interesting magazine of thought and fact,
published by Mr. Aitkin, *The United States Monthly Museum*.

Today the shop was empty except for a slightly built, red-
haired man of about thirty-eight who stood near the window
frowning over a copy of Adam Smith's *Theory of Moral Senti-
ments*. As soon as Benjamin picked up the latest issue of the
Monthly Museum, Mr. Aitkin brought the red-haired man over
to him.

"Dr. Rush," said the bookseller, "I would like you to meet
the new editor of the *Museum*, Mr. Thomas Paine."

The physician stretched out his hand cordially. "I am really
pleased to meet you, sir. You do excellently as editor of the
Museum. You must be experienced in this work."

Tom Paine had a bright and lively look. Now he laughed.
"Thank you, Doctor. No, actually I am a schoolmaster. I left
England for Philadelphia because Dr. Franklin gave me a letter
of recommendation to his family here. He thought they might
help me find a school near by."

"Be that as it may," Mr. Aitkin broke in, "he hung around
my bookshop so much, wearing out the books reading them,
that I judged he might as well work for me."

While Mr. Aitkin was speaking, Benjamin noticed that Tom
Paine was studying him carefully. After a moment Paine said
with some hesitation, "Sir, are you not the Dr. Rush who wrote

that splendid pamphlet, *Address to the Inhabitants of the British Colonies upon Slavekeeping?*"

"Why, yes, I am," Benjamin answered, pleased. "And now may I inquire, sir, was it not you who wrote the essay against slavery in the *Gazette?* Very sound reasoning, sir." Like many published letters and articles in those days, Paine's piece had been signed with some pen name like "Veritas" or "A Gentleman," so Benjamin wasn't sure of the author.

"Yes, it was I," Paine admitted. "I abhor the practice of slavery." It was clear that he and the doctor liked each other on sight.

"Good," Benjamin said. "So do I. Perhaps you would have dinner with me at my house tomorrow evening, and we can talk further? I live alone now, and we can talk freely."

The next evening Benjamin was delighted to learn that Tom Paine thought as he did—that the American colonies *must* secure complete independence from Britain. They talked about the subject all during the meal—from the "relish," which consisted of a slice of ham and a steak, to the soft, sweet flummery.

Finally the doctor asked, "Had you thought about writing a pamphlet on the subject, Mr. Paine?"

"Had you, Doctor?" Paine countered, trying, Benjamin thought, to read his eyes in the candlelight.

For a moment there was heavy silence. Both men knew the risks of such a publication—a charge of treason, with swift, severe punishment from the English.

Then Benjamin answered gravely, "Yes, I have considered it, sir. For months I have marshaled arguments for independence. I have them all down in my Commonplace Book."

"Well, why not, then?" There was a searching look on Paine's narrow face.

Benjamin absently smoothed back the lace on his cuff. Then

he sighed. "In truth, sir, I fear I have not yet quite got the courage. To talk is one thing. To publish, another. I know in my soul we must have independence. Yet the time to publish my belief never seems certain. Philadelphia is still largely Tory. An open written attack upon the Throne might well drive me from my practice—if not actually to prison. Or I think to myself, 'What if my pamphlet is not well received? What then? I am completely lost—with friends in no quarter.' "

To these remarks Tom Paine responded with downcast eyes and closed lips. For a few minutes the hiss of the logs burning in the fireplace was the only sound in the room.

Then Benjamin fixed a keen glance upon his guest. "But what about you, Mr. Paine? You are as strong for independence as I am. And you are a man alone, with no ties of family here. You can live anywhere in the colonies. How is your courage?"

Paine's eyes glowed bright. "My courage is in excellent health, Doctor. Such a pamphlet *is* needed. I will write it."

"Splendid! You may have all my notes on the subject."

Paine took Dr. Rush's notes home and studied them carefully. Later he told Benjamin that he found them so convincing that he wished to add them to the arguments he himself had gathered against British rule.

As he finished each section Paine read it to the doctor. Benjamin was elated with the way the schoolteacher-editor was presenting the case for freedom. He was glad, too, that Paine was writing at top speed, for events in the colonies were fast moving toward a showdown with the British.

In April, 1775, actual fighting broke out at Lexington and Concord. By May the vigorous Second Continental Congress was in session. And by June the colonists showed at Bunker Hill that they were further determined to stand up for their rights—with arms, if they had to. Now definitely, Benjamin believed, was the time for all Americans to stand united on the need for independence.

On the day that Tom Paine brought the final paragraphs to Benjamin for his opinion, he said, "I have thought of a name for the pamphlet. *Plain Talk.*"

"Hm-mmmm," reflected Benjamin. "I am not sure. It is plain talk, of course, but it is much more than that. It is plain good sense. Common sense. That's it," he stated with emphasis. "Call the pamphlet, 'Common Sense.' "

Common Sense was written, but its words of fire and truth would mean little, both men knew, if they remained hidden in Paine's desk. "Oh, that every colonist could read these words," Benjamin exclaimed with fervor.

"Agreed," Paine answered, "but where is the publisher brave enough to print them? You know that Robert Aitkin has already refused."

"Let me sound out certain patriots," Benjamin offered. He applied to one printer after another, but all were understandably afraid. Finally the doctor visited an eccentric Scotch bookseller and publisher named Robert Bell who had a shop on Third Street. Bell appeared to be afraid of nothing. In any case, he was a fearless Whig and always ready to shout in a loud voice that the colonies should be free of that —— king.

Benjamin handed him the manuscript of *Common Sense* to read. The material excited Bell so much that he said he would get it out quicker than a redcoat could fix his bayonet. While the Scotsman's enthusiasm burned bright, Benjamin hurried Paine over to Bell's shop.

In a few weeks, on January 10, 1776, *Common Sense* appeared—published anonymously.

Good as he had known Paine's pamphlet to be, even Benjamin was astonished by its effect. He doubted if a single person in the colonies had missed reading it or had at least heard it read. All that winter people talked about *Common Sense* in their homes and discussed it in the inns. School children recited it in class, and ministers preached it as a sermon from their pulpits. Newspapers openly quoted it in their columns.

In a few weeks this little pamphlet converted thousands of colonists to a belief in the cause of American independence—a belief which only a few weeks earlier they had considered to be high treason.

As he delightedly viewed this effect, Benjamin Rush remarked, "Some of the arguments in the pamphlet perhaps are mine, but the words are Paine's. It is to the American fortune that it was he who had the courage to write and publish *Common Sense*."

About the time that Benjamin was helping Paine with *Common Sense*, an event took place which planted the seed of worry in his mind. It began one foggy December night in 1775 when a tall, aristocratic-looking man strode impatiently into his office.

Benjamin looked up from the tiny brass scales upon which he was weighing snakeroot powder. "Dr. Morgan!" he exclaimed in surprise. "I thought you were in Cambridge with the American troops. How goes the siege at Boston?"

"Well enough, I believe—from the military standpoint. We have the British pretty well bottled up in the city." Dr. Morgan sank heavily into a chair and impatiently dashed his cocked hat to the floor.

"Then what is wrong?" Benjamin asked with a sympathy he usually reserved for his patients. Perhaps, he thought as he observed his visitor's tense lips, my friend is ill.

Dr. Morgan eyed him intently. "Have you heard nothing

from the Adamses or others among your friends in the Congress?"

"Why, no," Benjamin replied, puzzled by Morgan's manner. "Certain of them have asked me to use my knowledge as a chemist to investigate the quality of our American powder manufactories, but that is all. Is there trouble with the Medical Department?"

Dr. Morgan sighed wearily. "Trouble is too mild a word for this situation, Ben. If the Congress will not support me with a strong hand, I know not what to do."

"Why should the Congress not support you?" Benjamin demanded. "Surely the members know they were fortunate in securing a man of your mark to be Director General. Especially after the Dr. Church—er—incident."

By the "Dr. Church incident," Benjamin meant the unhappy fact that Dr. Benjamin Church of Boston, the first Director General of the Army Medical Department, had served only three months—when he was found guilty of treason and dismissed.

"Yes, I know," Morgan smiled wryly, "but to listen to the regimental surgeons, one would think that it is I who am the enemy—not the British. They war upon me night and day."

"How so?" As Ben studied his friend's sensitive, intelligent face, he thought to himself that in all the colonies the Congress could have found no man abler, braver or more dedicated to his duty than John Morgan of Philadelphia. What then could be causing the difficulty with the regimental surgeons?

Suddenly, and for no clear reason, he remembered that just last week Dr. Billy Shippen had stopped him in Pine Street and inquired whether he had heard lately from Dr. Morgan. Benjamin had thought at the time that Shippen's eyes had a strange gleam. But since he himself could make nothing of the remark, he had forgotten the episode—until now.

Morgan, sunk in the gloom of his thoughts, appeared not to have heard his question. "What about the regimental surgeons, Doctor?" Benjamin prodded gently.

With a sound of impatience, Morgan jumped to his feet and began to pace the floor. "Briefly, Ben, the regimental surgeons are—impossible. I fear that when heavy fighting comes, they will be completely unequal to the situation.

"To begin with," Morgan went on, "most of them are ignorant and untrained. And they refuse to submit to an examination so that the Medical Department may weed out the most incompetent. They declare that neither Congress nor anyone appointed by Congress—that means me and the other officers of the Medical Department—has any authority over them. They maintain they will take orders only from their own state legislatures or from officers appointed by these state legislatures.

"So consequently," Morgan continued angrily, "they pay no attention to the rules laid down by the Army Medical Department for the care of the sick and wounded. And they are upheld in this dangerous disobedience by the military officers of their regiments. Of course these men received their appointments from the state legislatures, too."

Benjamin frowned. "This could certainly become serious if we have large numbers of sick and wounded to care for."

"Exactly." Dr. Morgan banged a chair for emphasis. "That is why I am in Philadelphia—to explain the situation to the Congress. That body must show some strength. It must set down in writing the responsibilities and authority of the Medical Department. Why even now the regimental surgeons demand drugs and surgical instruments from the Medical Department's meager supply. God knows where we will procure these supplies later on, now that we can no longer easily bring them in from Europe."

Abruptly the storm of anger passed from John Morgan, leaving him pale and worn looking.

"Oh, there's a lot more to tell, Ben," he said dispiritedly, "but I cannot take the time now. I go to find Sam Adams—he is Chairman of the Medical Committee, isn't he? He has not answered a one of my letters, but perhaps I can get something out of him in person."

Benjamin nodded and walked thoughtfully with his friend to the front gate. Privately, he had determined to hunt up Sam Adams, too. It was absurd that a group of ignorant backwoods physicians, who didn't know the first thing about military medicine, should block the path of a man who had been an army doctor in the French and Indian War and had studied with the masters of military medicine abroad. Absurd—and perilous to the whole American army.

The sun had barely risen the next morning when Benjamin tapped at the lodgings of Samuel Adams, influential congressman from Massachusetts.

Adams was dressed and adjusting his stock when Benjamin, apologizing for his early call, entered his bedchamber.

"Do not bother to explain," Adams said in his brusque way. "I know why you are here. Dr. Morgan cornered me last night."

"Cornered you," Benjamin echoed with disapproval. "Why the man is Director General of the Army Medical Department. He has a right to see you. His problem is grave."

"I suppose so," Adams flung out irritably, "but it is not a pressing problem at the moment. What soldiers we have are healthy, well fed and sufficiently clad. Hang it, Rush, can you not see that the urgent thing that faces us now is getting together the men, supplies and ammunition—the very instruments of war itself? Now look, I am chairman of twenty-three other committees and a member of ninety altogether. I have no time to bother with these letters of complaint which pour in."

"Letters of complaint? From whom?"

"Well, of course Morgan keeps writing me. But most of the Congress receives letters from the regimental surgeons and from the colonels of the regiments denouncing Morgan's dictatorial methods. I wish the whole pack and parcel of them would settle the thing 'mongst themselves. As for me, I know not who is right."

"Dr. Morgan is right," Benjamin said quietly. "If he seems dictatorial, 'tis only that he wishes to build a competent Medical Department while there is yet time."

"Well, then," Sam Adams turned for a final glare before he stamped out of the room. "Perhaps he sets about presenting his ideas in the wrong way. The junior Dr. Shippen indicated as much to me just last week."

"The junior Doctor Shippen!" Benjamin repeated under his breath.

All at once he believed he understood the meaning of the gleam in Billy Shippen's eyes.

CHAPTER EIGHT

Julia

During that same fateful year of 1775 Dr. Benjamin Rush experienced what he called the greatest blessing of his life. One morning in August just as the sun was coming up over the Delaware, Benjamin awoke and stretched his arms and legs mightily. Yawning, he sat up and rumpled his hair. From his window he could see a thin, whitish haze on the river. "Another hot, sticky Philadelphia day," he concluded with mild disapproval.

Then with a surge of pleasure he remembered. This was the day he was going to Princeton to visit Judge Stockton and his family, whom he had not seen for several years.

Outside his window a cart loaded with golden peaches rumbled past on the way to the market. The sight of the fruit made Benjamin hurry even more. How pleasant it would be, he thought, to stroll over the wide meadows and the gently rolling hills near his old college.

The afternoon found him on his newly bought black mare Diamond, galloping northeast on the dusty road toward Princeton. When two days later Diamond trotted up the long, tree-lined drive to Morven, Judge and Mrs. Stockton were waiting on the columned porch to welcome him. Behind them stood a slender, brown-haired girl who lowered her dark eyes shyly when the young doctor bounded to the porch.

"Come in, come in," boomed the Judge. "It is good to see you."

"Indeed it is," Mrs. Stockton added. "You are just in time for tea."

Benjamin's glance went to the girl. How soft and appealing was her expression, and he was sure he had never seen a lovelier complexion.

"Can this young lady be—?" he began.

"It can and is," Richard Stockton answered with a smile. "You remember my eldest daughter Julia, do you not?"

"I do indeed." Dr. Rush looked directly at the girl. "Did I not once hold her in my arms?" There was a teasing sparkle in his blue eyes.

"Oh, sir," Julia blushed becomingly, as her parents laughed. "I was but a child of two when I fell into your path at the college commencement."

"And now you are a charming young lady." Benjamin was not aware that admiration showed so clearly in his voice, but Judge and Mrs. Stockton glanced meaningly at each other.

The visit raced by. To Benjamin it seemed that his thoughts were always in a happy haze about Julia. Julia with pink cheeks and bouncing curls as she rode horseback through the countryside with him. Julia playing her lute and singing a Scottish ballad in a sweet contralto voice. Julia . . . Julia.

He could scarcely bear to leave her but he knew his patients were waiting for him. Then when he was back in Philadelphia and writing notes on his cases, he found himself daydreaming. He remembered the sweetness in Julia's dark eyes, the fascinating little lisp in her speech. She was intelligent, too, he thought fondly. Once her shyness was overcome, how cleverly she talked about the books she was reading and the sermons she had heard.

Well it was no use trying to put Julia out of his mind, Benjamin realized. He couldn't do it. He had to see her again. Tossing aside the notes of Jabez Blake's autumnal fever, he wrote Judge Stockton for permission to pay court to his daughter.

As soon as the permission arrived by post, Benjamin saddled Diamond and galloped again to Morven. He went again and again, and then he wrote in his Commonplace Book, "My suit has been blessed with success."

In January, 1776, he and Julia were married. The bride was sixteen and Dr. Benjamin Rush had just turned thirty.

The first months of marriage brought unaccustomed duties to Julia. Helping her husband receive his patients and serving as hostess to the numerous visitors who came to talk about the growing war soon tired her. In May, she decided to go to Morven for a visit.

Benjamin missed her intensely. No matter how busy he was, almost every night he sat at the mahogany table in his parlor and penned his young wife a letter. Often they were long and newsy, like this one of May 27, 1776.

My dearest:

How blessings brighten as they take their flight. I did not know till since we parted how much you were part of myself, and I did feel some abatement of my affection for my country when I reflect that even she has deprived me of an hour of my dear Julia's company. I have more than once forgotten that you were out of town and have come in from visiting my patients prepared to entertain you with an account of everything I had seen and heard in my walks—and then alas, the first steps I took in passing through the entry convinced me of my mistake. . . .

Friday. Mrs. Hancock (wife of the President of the Continental Congress) called to pay her compliments to

our Aunt Boudinot. I called on General Washington. I
then spent all afternoon at home. I had a visit from Col.
Lee who drank tea with me. We talked of nothing but
the base defection of the Maryland Convention from the
late resolve of Congress. The Colonel said he should hate
hereafter to breathe the contaminated air of that province
on his way to Virginia.

Saturday. Was called up at 6 to visit patient near Frankford—came home before 9 and was favored with a visit
from Dr. Treat of Burlington and Mr. Rittenhouse [noted
mathematician and astronomer, active in the Revolutionary
government of Pennsylvania.] Latter breakfasted with me.

Sunday. Awoke—but no Julia near me. I wafted a sigh
after her to Morven. Inoculated a New England officer
recommended to me by General Mifflin. . . . Was just preparing to go to church when was sent for to pay another
visit to my patient near Frankford. Met Mrs. Bache [Ben-
jamin Franklin's daughter] this evening in the street who
told me she called upon you yesterday but did not leave
name. Came in at 9 and sat down at southeast corner of
our common parlor to write to you.

Tomorrow General Washington is to review all our city
battalions. The design of this is to give the Indian ambas-
sadors now among us an august idea of the military
strength of our province.

Adieu, my sweet girl. Take care of your health and keep
up your spirits. Use as little vinegar as possible in your
diet and leave off thinking of cargoes of Hessians and
Hanoverians that are on the way to fight against us. All is
for the best. God bless you, my dear Angel. My best affec-
tions await the whole family. Yours most affectionately,

Benjamin Rush

Julia must have been quite a letter writer, too, because two days later her devoted husband sent her this note.

My dearest Life—I have wept over both your letters. I thank you for your tender regard for my welfare in the first, and I rejoice to discover such a flow of spirits in the second of them. Our cause prospers in every county of the province. The hand of heaven is with us. Did I not think so, I would not have embarked in it. You have everything to hope and nothing to fear from the part which duty to God, to my country, and to my conscience have led me to take in our affairs. . . . Entertained Mr. Rittenhouse, Col. Trumbull, and Major Mifflin with a plain family dinner. . . . Adieu, my sweet Julia. My heart glows with an affection for you at this instant so tender, so delicate, and so refined that I want words to express it. . . . I think, write, talk, work, love—all, all—only for you. Yours,

BR

All that spring of 1776 Dr. Rush mingled constantly with the more radical members of the Second Continental Congress —the ones who wanted a definite break with England. He had them to his house for breakfast, dinner and tea. He met with them at various taverns around Philadelphia. Once Congressman Duer of New York told him that the King of England had hired seventeen thousand mercenary troops from Germany to fight the colonists.

"Think of it," Duer said. "The Landgrave of Hesse-Cassel has sold his Hessians to the British for thirty marks a head— with the understanding that he will receive thirty more for each man killed, wounded or captured."

Benjamin shrugged. "Thirty marks to the Landgrave! What

kind of soldiers do you think those poor Hessians will make—
in a battle of free men fighting for their freedom?"

On July 15, 1776, Benjamin himself was elected to the
Congress by the radical group of Pennsylvania Whigs. The
Declaration of Independence had already been passed on July
4th, but his election gave Dr. Rush the prized opportunity of
signing this great document. He did so on August 2, 1776—
along with forty others.

As he placed his neat signature next to Robert Morris', his
heart so pounded with emotion that he felt suffocated. Two
days later he watched his father-in-law Richard Stockton, a
delegate to the Congress from New Jersey, also sign the Declaration. Both men were said to have shed tears of joy at the great
privilege which had been granted them.

Even though the signing of the Declaration of Independence
gave the colonists a feeling of unity and a clearer understanding of what they were fighting for, events did not go well for
the young American army that fall and winter of 1776.

In early March when General Washington's troops seized
Dorchester Heights outside of Boston, the British sailed away
to Nova Scotia to wait for reinforcements. Then Washington
took his poorly armed and ill-trained militiamen to New York
to stop the British when they came back—as he knew they
would.

By July the British were ready to return. Waiting for them
was a larger group of Americans than they had left. Now along
with the New Englanders and the soldiers from the Middle
Colonies stood the Virginia and Carolina sharpshooters. The
patriot soldiers had cheered when they saw the long, wicked-
looking rifles the southerners were carrying. But unfortunately

the newcomers had brought with them more than powerful rifles. They had brought the deadly germs of disease.

In colonial times, traveling was so difficult that most people never journeyed far from home. In their home area they managed to build up resistance to the few diseases peculiar to their region. They did not, however, develop resistance to sicknesses from other places.

Thus when they came as soldiers to Washington's New York camp, and for the first time mingled with men from other regions, they fell ready victims to a variety of infections. Soon typhus, typhoid, smallpox and dysentery raced from brigade to brigade. Within three months one third of Washington's army was sick. And this was even before a major battle was fought.

Most of the sick still lay in the regimental hospitals which, as Dr. Morgan had told Benjamin, were not real hospitals at all. They were merely a collection of the regiment's sick placed in some house, barn or other building. They had no beds or other equipment. Instead each patient spread his own blanket on the floor on the top of straw which often already crawled with lice from other patients.

The regimental surgeons were not prepared for a sudden deluge of sick men. Now they realized what they were up against. With their stock of drugs mostly gone and many of their patients dying from infected limbs because they lacked knives suitable for amputation, they understood what Dr. Morgan had been talking about. Frantically they begged Morgan and the Army Medical Department for help. But Congress had not provided adequately for the general hospitals either. Tragically, the Army Medical Department doctors were not much better off than were the regimental surgeons.

Dr. Rush first learned of this deplorable situation when he was called on by Dr. Binney, whom Dr. Morgan had sent to

Philadelphia in a desperate effort to locate surgical instruments.

"What instruments have you been able to buy?" asked Benjamin.

"None whatever," Dr. Binney replied gloomily. "The only workmen who are skilled enough to make them have been ordered by the Congress to manufacture arms instead."

"I know," Benjamin answered. "I am afraid my own plea in Congress has fallen upon deaf ears. Is Dr. Morgan still with the Long Island camp?"

"Heaven knows where that driven man is," Binney answered with a despairing shake of his head. "He tries with superhuman effort to outfit the hospitals, and when he can spare a few days from this and from tending the sick with his own hands, he gallops hundreds of miles in a search for medicines. He even personally begs housewives for the gift of an old knife or a linen sheet which can be made into bandages. By the way," Binney reached into his tunic for a letter, "Dr. Morgan asked me to show you this communication from Dr. Jonathan Potts at Fort George."

Benjamin knew that his old friend of Edinburgh days was with the American army which had been so successful in Canada—successful until they were stricken with disease.

Now with a worried expression he read Dr. Potts' words:

"The distressing situation of the sick here is not to be described—without clothing, without bedding, or shelter sufficient to keep them from the weather . . . we have at present upwards of a thousand sick, crowded into sheds and laboring under the various and cruel disorders of dysenteries, bilious putrid fevers, and the effects of confluent smallpox. . . . To treat these seriously sick men," Dr. Potts wrote, "I have only four surgeons and four surgeon's mates, and my medicines are nearly exhausted."

"Dear God," Benjamin murmured, genuinely shocked. "The Congress *must* hear of this." He paused for a moment in thought, then said, "As soon as I can arrange my affairs here, I shall journey to the New York camp and talk with Dr. Morgan himself."

CHAPTER NINE

The Heroic Doctor Morgan

The weeks went by, however, with Congress taking no action in the matter and Benjamin unable to get away to visit Dr. Morgan in New York. Like the other members of Congress, he was busy helping direct the war effort. He had little time now for his practice. Most of his waking hours were spent as a chemist investigating and remedying the defects of American gunpowder factories which were completely inadequate for the Army's needs. Julia complained she scarcely ever saw him.

Once when he returned from such a mission, he heard that in his absence Congress had appointed Dr. Billy Shippen, Jr. to be Director of the Flying Camp (field hospital) in New Jersey. This position did not, however, Benjamin observed, keep Shippen away very much from Philadelphia. As a matter of fact, Dr. Billy always seemed to be somewhere around the State House, laughing and chatting with the congressmen. Often he invited a number of them to dinner at his big, beautiful home. Usually these dinners included his father and his two brothers-in-law, the Lees of Virginia, all of whom were in Congress, too.

Dr. Rush wished that Dr. Shippen's unconcern about his field hospital duties meant that things were going well for the young American army. Reports from New York, however, showed heartbreakingly otherwise. The Americans had been badly defeated at Long Island, but few people were surprised by this. After all, the British had a splendidly equipped and trained army of twenty-seven thousand men, while Washington had only seventeen thousand, part of whom were untrained militia, and thirty-seven hundred of whom were sick.

The report of the retreat itself gave Benjamin a feeling almost of despair. "Everything," he read, "was confusion when the sick and wounded were ferried across the East River in a heavy rain; sufferers were landed at different wharves and carried without thought to the nearest houses. It took Dr. Morgan and his assistants all night to find them and transport them to hospitals."

To make matters worse, discouragement had affected discipline. Although officers assigned soldiers to help in the hospitals, most of these assignees deserted during the night and returned to their regiments. Many of the sick escaped and wandered into the country to spread disease throughout the land.

Although Benjamin knew that Dr. Morgan had not wanted to place the sick and wounded in the ill-equipped regimental hospitals, he now learned that Morgan had had no choice.

Some weeks earlier the Director General had established a new general hospital at Newark, which he had managed to outfit with a few medicines and supplies. But when the time came to move the casualties to Newark, Morgan found that in their anxiety to escape, the militiamen had taken the wagons in which he planned to evacuate the sick. With his wagons gone, Morgan had been forced to crowd the sick and wounded into unsuitable barns, houses and outbuildings at Kingsbridge and Harlem Heights—under the care of the regimental surgeons.

From Kingsbridge, Dr. Tilton, the surgeon, wrote so disturbing a report that an angry flush rose to Benjamin's thin cheeks as he read: "The camp is indescribably filthy. All manner of excrementitious matter is scattered indiscriminately throughout the camp so that there is a disagreeable smell everywhere. Sometimes there are no ovens, and flour is served instead of bread. Some soldiers try to bake bread on hot stones, and others in ashes. As a result, many become afflicted with jaundice. Of the Army with Washington on the east side of the river," Dr. Tilton concluded, ". . . there are 15,105 fit for duty. Of the total sick, there are 7,610."

Benjamin crushed Dr. Tilton's report into his coat pocket and dashed over to the State House. Perhaps he could find the Adamses or John Hancock or James Wilson or some other influential member of Congress and get action on money and supplies for the hard-pressed Army Medical Department.

A chill October wind blew on his angry face as he hurried through the Walnut Street gate. He checked his step briefly to watch Dr. Billy Shippen and his two brothers-in-law saunter through the portal. Shippen was looking very pleased with himself, Benjamin noted—and wondered why.

After a search he located the Adamses and three other congressmen in a huddle in the State Assembly room upstairs.

"We know all about the sickness in the Army," one congressman replied irritably when Benjamin had had his say. "And if we don't watch our tongues, the British will find out just how weak we are."

"Aye," said another, "we have trouble enough holding the men in the ranks as it is, without all these alarums about the hospitals. If you ask me, Dr. Morgan stirs up dissension among his staff by his high-handed demands for impossible perfection. Perhaps some other director general—" he stopped, then said abruptly to Benjamin, "Have you checked the powder manufactory near Baltimore?"

Benjamin stared at the congressmen in astonishment. "The manufactory can wait," he snapped. "I fear you gentlemen have no idea of the difficulties Dr. Morgan labors under." Then in an angry tone he announced, "I shall leave for Dr. Morgan's headquarters within the week. Perhaps as a member of the Medical Committee, my personal observation will be useful to this body." He whirled around and strode off, leaving behind him an unfriendly mutter of conversation.

All through the early fall of 1776 General Washington's forces had been retreating toward New Jersey. They were followed slowly but relentlessly by the well-trained, well-cared-for troops of General Howe. As the Americans withdrew, Dr. Morgan tried to prepare for their future needs by opening a general hospital at Hackensack, New Jersey.

It was here that Benjamin first sought the Director General. As he slid off his horse in front of the large wooden building, he was met by an elderly man whom he recognized as a doctor he had known in his own apprentice days.

"Where is Dr. Morgan?" Benjamin asked, gazing around with disapproval at the shedlike building which did not have even a wooden floor.

"Oh, for the love of heaven, can you not let Dr. Morgan rest awhile?" the man burst out. "He fell in exhaustion upon the ground not an hour ago—and was promptly asleep. After all, how much can one man do?"

Benjamin coughed as he felt the raw damp of the unheated building. "What do you mean?" All at once he realized with dismay that nearly a thousand men were lying around him in the cold shed.

" 'Tis this," said the other doctor. "The day Dr. Morgan arrived here, three hundred sick and wounded from the New York engagements were brought to him, although he was quite

alone. In a few days there were over a thousand. The building
was not yet finished—as you see—and he had no bread, flour
or fresh provisions. He attended to the seriously wounded at
once—trepanning skulls and amputating limbs, while he sent
off dispatch riders for help. He had not even orderlies to help
with the menial chores," the man finished in a dull voice. "It
was only this morning that four doctors and several orderlies
arrived to assist him. Wait!" the older man peered toward the
back of the building, "I think Dr. Morgan stands up."

"Thank you, Doctor!" Benjamin ran toward his old friend,
holding out his hand. "Dr. Morgan, sir. It distresses me to find
you like this."

The Director General straightened his tired body. "I apolo-
gize for my appearance, sir," he said, indicating his stained,
rumpled uniform, "but I have not had my clothes off for a
week."

"I understand," said Benjamin, "but now you must rest.
Perhaps I can help in your place."

"No." Morgan was impatient. "I must ride to Fort Lee to
ask General Greene about supplies for the hospital here. Will
you come with me?"

When Drs. Rush and Morgan arrived at Fort Lee, they
found that General Greene had a visitor—Dr. Billy Shippen.

As usual, Shippen appeared well rested and well dressed. He
held out his hand to his "old friend." "You look thin, Morgan,"
he said. "I hope you have not been ill."

Then to the astonishment of both Benjamin and Morgan he
continued, "By the way, what are you doing here? I am in
control in New Jersey, you know. You belong in New York."

John Morgan's tired eyes looked blank. With a nervous edge
to his voice he said coldly, "I am in no mood for jest, Doctor.

I am the Medical Director. I belong throughout the American states."

Shippen raised his eyebrows. "Perhaps," he said with a meaning smile, "you had better question the Congress about that."

Morgan turned to Benjamin. "You are in Congress," he said. "What does he mean?"

"Let me answer for Congressman Rush," Shippen intervened, "since he was out of the city when the action was taken. Or so my dispatch rider has just told me. In short, Dr. Morgan, the Congress has given me complete charge of all the hospitals west of the Hudson River. Your authority is confined to the hospitals east of that river. And since, even as we speak, General Washington retreats ever westward, soon—if I may say so, sir, you will be a director general with little to direct."

Benjamin gasped, but Morgan, swaying on his feet, appeared too weary to comprehend. "An absurd situation," he murmured through pale lips, "but its discussion can wait. My business with General Greene is more urgent."

On the way back to Hackensack, however, Morgan suddenly remarked, "Ben, that statement of Shippen's about my authority being limited to New York. Can it be true?" he asked indignantly. "The Congress knows Shippen has had no experience in military medicine. What do you make of it?"

"I do not know," said Benjamin honestly. "Perhaps the dispatch rider brought inaccurate information. As far as I know, you are still Director General. So carry on as usual. I shall, however, return to Philadelphia and look into the matter at once."

But when he again reached Philadelphia, he learned that Billy Shippen was right. Congress *had* appointed Shippen Director of all the hospitals west of the Hudson River, and Mor-

gan, Director only of those east of it. It was incredible, but
true.

What a pity, Benjamin thought, that while John Morgan
was toiling on the battlefields, and riding hundreds of miles on
horseback to gather supplies—overseeing the building of hospitals, instructing incompetent surgeons and doing surgery
with his own hands—while he was doing all these things, Dr.
Shippen was busy in Philadelphia ingratiating himself with
Congress. Ingratiating himself and—Benjamin reflected bitterly
—plotting revenge upon the man who, he believed, had robbed
him of his glory as the founder of the first medical school in
America.

As October's brilliant days turned to the gray ones of November, the plight of Washington's troops grew more dismal.
Supplies of vitally needed gunpowder were dangerously low.
Certain Americans were in France negotiating for shipments of
the powder, but Dr. Rush still tried to step up the quality and
output of the local supply.

One bleak afternoon as he was inspecting a powder mill
north of the city, a man on horseback galloped up to him.

"Oh, sir," the man cried in an agitated voice, "are you not
Dr. Rush, the son-in-law of Judge Stockton of Princeton?"

"I am, sir, what is it?" The doctor's face was already grim.

As soon as Benjamin heard what the man had to say, he
wheeled his own horse around and dashed back to Philadelphia. He must talk to Julia at once.

Hours later when he reined his horse in front of his house,
he could see Julia in the kitchen garden transplanting a few
late herbs into a flowerpot. He tied his horse to the hitching
post and put a calm look on his face before he hurried to her.

"Julia, my dear girl," he said in a gentle voice as he reached for her hand, "come into the house. I have something to tell you."

Julia's dark eyes went anxiously to his face. "What is wrong, Benjamin?"

"Try to be brave, my angel," the doctor drew his wife close. "Your father has been taken by the British. They have beaten him badly and carried him to the prison in New York."

Julia's lips looked dry. "What of my mother?" she whispered.

"Your mother is well. She was not with your father at the time. But Morven is plundered and its gardens destroyed. They have burnt your father's furniture and his books. And all the cattle, pigs and other stock have been led away to feed the British army."

Julia stared at him with stricken eyes.

"Julia, Julia, don't look like that," Benjamin tried to comfort her. "The Congress will see that your father is freed." But his young wife didn't hear him. She had fallen in his arms in a faint.

Benjamin rushed for his medicine chest. A whiff of sal ammoniac was what she needed. In a few moments she opened her eyes. For the rest of the afternoon she seemed composed and hopeful about her father's fate.

That night after they had blown out the bedroom candles, Julia told her husband she thought by midsummer they would be having a little son or daughter. Benjamin was so happy to hear the news that it was not until morning that he felt some concern over the shock Julia had received regarding her father.

By the end of the first week in December, 1776, Benjamin, together with the other members of Congress, realized that Sir William Howe was going to try to take Philadelphia.

"Perhaps," one congressman remarked, "General Washington can hold off these well-trained troops with his inexperienced ones. Perhaps he cannot. In any case, it will never do for the Congress to risk being captured by the British. If that happens, we are all done for."

"Well," said practical Samuel Adams, "let us leave Philadelphia and meet elsewhere."

His motion was passed quickly, and Congress decided to leave their first capital and meet twelve days later in Baltimore.

As soon as the day's session was over, Benjamin hurried home, through the back alley into the kitchen. Betsey, their combination maid and cook, was polishing a silver tureen. "Don't bother with silver polishing now, Betsey," the doctor said. "Just find something to pack the silver in. We shall take it with us."

"Why, where are we going?" called Julia, hastening in from the parlor where she had been embroidering. She looked anxious.

"Oh," Benjamin was casual, "I think it might be a good idea for you to stay with Cousin Elisha Hall for a while. You will be safe there—out in the Maryland countryside."

"Safe. Safe from what?" Julia's eyes were widening.

"Well, they say," Benjamin's voice was carefully level, "that the British may take Philadelphia soon. I think you'd best not be here—especially now."

"Oh, Ben," Julia flung herself upon him. "You must leave, too. Remember what happened to Papa. And you signed the Declaration of Independence, just as he did. They'll be after you. Please, *please* come with me." She tugged at his shoulders.

"Now, my angel," Benjamin said with gentle firmness as he took her hands from his coat. "You know you would not want me to hide away like a coward. Come, get your things together. William will be around directly with the chair."

After Benjamin had deposited his unusually quiet young wife at Colonel Hall's plantation in Cecil County, he rode hastily back to the Walnut Street house and packed his books and part of his furniture. These he took for safekeeping to the home of a farmer who lived over by the Schuylkill River. Then stuffing his medicine chest with all the supplies it would hold, he rode out to join the Pennsylvania militia at Bristol. The militia (similar to our present-day national guard) had been ordered out to reinforce General Washington's army in its effort to save the city.

On Christmas Eve, 1776, Benjamin visited General Washington at his Delaware headquarters near the Delaware River. To the doctor's observing eye, the General looked worried and depressed.

"Ah, Dr. Rush," Washington said sadly, "my army is ragged and dissolving. So many men go home the instant their three-month enlistment is up." As he spoke he tore up a piece of paper on which he had been writing. One of the scraps fell to the floor near Benjamin's feet.

"I understand, sir," Dr. Rush reassured the General. "But Congress well knows your difficulties and distresses. Rest assured it will support you to the limit of its ability." His eye was struck with the inscription upon the scrap of paper. It read "Victory or Death."

About midnight, Benjamin left again for Bristol. It was bitter cold and snowing heavily. Great pieces of floating ice rocked about in the river. A vicious night not fit for man or beast to be out in, he thought, pitying the poorly clad Continental soldiers.

Two mornings later Benjamin was astonished to hear that

General Washington had on that very night surprised and captured one thousand Hessian soldiers at Trenton. The countersign of his troops had been "Victory or Death," the writing on the scrap of paper. The doctor was filled with admiration. Even in the depth of despair Washington had been able to plan this master stroke.

On January 2nd, the British and American armies fought again, and the American army withdrew. Benjamin had planned to go along with it, but now all around him on the battlefield wounded men groaned for help.

One young soldier staggered toward him. His right hand hung a little above the wrist, held by nothing but a piece of skin. "Cannon ball hit me," the boy moaned.

Benjamin looked about hastily. Just over the first hill was a small house. "Carry this man there," he ordered two other soldiers. "And bring in any others needing attention. We will use the house as a hospital."

By evening, twenty wounded men had been brought to the little house. Benjamin, aided by a New Jersey doctor named Cochran, dressed their wounds as best he could, with practically no supplies on hand.

"It was then, and for the first time," he wrote later, "that war appeared to me in its awful plentitude of horrors. We all lay down on some straw in the same room with our wounded patients. I want words to describe the anguish of my soul, excited by the cries and groans and convulsions of the men who lay by my side. I slept two or three hours.

"About four o'clock, Dr. Cochran went up to Trenton to inquire for our army. He returned in haste and said they were not to be found. We now procured wagons, and after putting our patients in them, directed that they should follow us to

Bordentown to which place we supposed our army had retreated."

But Washington's army had not gone to Bordentown. Instead Washington had fought and outwitted Lord Cornwallis at Princeton. When Benjamin reached that place, the battlefield near the town was still red with blood and filled with the shrieking of wounded men from both sides.

Again Drs. Rush and Cochran set about doing what they could. This time they saw a number of British surgeon's mates trying to gather the injured into one place so that their own army doctors could look at them later. Order and discipline—that is how the British Army Medical Department works, Benjamin thought enviously as he tried with an old shirt to stanch the flow of blood from a soldier's side. That is how it should be. His eyes went pityingly to the young soldier he was attending. "So Dr. Shippen is in charge here," he muttered angrily, "well, where are our own army doctors and medical supplies now?"

Just before sundown Benjamin was able to leave the wounded men for a short while. Through the cold, damp air he rode to the village of Princeton. Here his heart sank. The lovely homes, the churches, part of the college—all stood in ruin—burnt and destroyed by the British. He decided to see if Julia's girlhood home had been spared, and turned his horse on the road toward Morven. Before he had gone far, he passed an emaciated, pitiful-looking man limping up the road.

Startled, Benjamin reined in his horse, then jumped down. The man was Richard Stockton. "Sir!" Benjamin exclaimed, astonished. "We heard you were in prison at New York."

"I was," Judge Stockton replied in a dull voice, as though he was still dazed from shock, "but I am out on parole. The British have exchanged me for a wealthy Tory."

With a strong but gentle hand, Benjamin lifted his father-in-law to his horse. Then he led the animal up the road to Morven. They found the beautiful mansion deserted and ransacked of everything, but still standing. The Judge almost wept with relief to be there, and insisted he would be comfortable and happy. Ben was not to worry, but go on with his own plans. Ah, now I have good news to take to Julia, Benjamin thought, pleased, especially that her father is out of prison.

Shortly afterward he snatched a few days with Julia at Colonel Hall's Maryland plantation. Then he set off for Baltimore to attend to his duties in Congress. He arrived about the middle of January, 1777. As he was dismounting from his horse in front of the hall where Congress was meeting, a proud-looking man with burning dark eyes stepped forward to greet him. For a moment Benjamin did not recognize the gaunt figure. Then he exclaimed in an incredulous tone, "Dr. Morgan! Is it really you?"

Morgan smiled sardonically. "Yes, I suppose circumstances have altered my appearance. You have heard of my dismissal from the Army Medical Department, of course?"

"Dismissal!" Benjamin repeated, shocked. "Indeed I had not. When, for heaven's sake?"

"On ninth, January. Congress turned me out without holding hearings or without consulting General Washington on the matter."

At first Benjamin stared, speechless at this unjust act of Congress. Then his words came in a torrent.

"What a miscarriage of justice! It should be apparent to a child that you accomplished a great deal in an impossible situation. It is true that the Medical Department frequently failed this past year. But then so did every department in the Army fail—the quartermaster, the commissary, the military itself.

Hang it, Doctor, we are all amateurs pitted against professionals. The remarkable thing is that we have kept steadfast in the face of almost continual defeat."

"Be that as it may," Morgan answered gloomily, "I still feel that I have been unfairly held up to public disgrace. I cannot rest until I have collected enough testimony to prove that my administration was a good one. Can I count on your aid, Benjamin?"

Dr. Rush impulsively stretched out both his hands. "As of this moment, Dr. Morgan," he said warmly. "As of now."

CHAPTER TEN

More Dangerous Than the Enemy

One day at the end of January, 1777, a stinging snow bit into the face of Dr. Benjamin Rush as he guided his horse toward the huge Brethren's House at Bethlehem, Pennsylvania. By early gray dusk he reached the great, barnlike structure which was now the main hospital for the sick of General Washington's army.

Within its gray stone walls lay seven hundred sick soldiers, although there was scarce room for three hundred. They had been brought there in open wagons, often with snow and icy rain pelting down and through their ragged clothing. Some had died from exposure while awaiting removal from the wagons.

At first when they saw the soldiers' half-starved bodies and filthy rags swarming with lice, the kindhearted Moravians of Bethlehem had turned away their heads to hide the shock and pity in their eyes. Then they had set about collecting what food, blankets, jackets, shoes and breeches they could. But there wasn't much they could do about providing beds for these sick. Straw perhaps, but not beds.

When he stepped inside the building, Benjamin immediately noticed that in several instances three sufferers lay upon one pallet of straw. Faint gleams from candles showed gaunt faces with dry tongues licking parched lips. One of the faces called for water, and a barefoot orderly—his own shirt in strings—carried a dripping cup toward the sick boy.

Benjamin's eyes fell to the pallet of the youth who lay nearest him. Even in the dim light he could see vermin crawling. The youth was too ill to notice the lice, but William Smith, a hospital doctor, came forward out of the shadows and whispered.

" 'Tis clear, Doctor, that straw should have been changed long ago. Four patients already have died upon it, but we have so little help, and there is no order, no discipline here. The men do as they please."

Appalled, Benjamin shook his head. He did not know, of course—no one did in 1777—that it was the lice which carried the deadly typhus from one man to another, even from the dead to the living. But simple cleanliness in a hospital—everyone understood that was important!

Dr. Smith appeared to read his mind. "The place *is* filthy, Doctor. But we do not have even brooms. Half the staff is sick. Several of the doctors, nurses and orderlies already have died from hospital fever." Suddenly his face brightened. "Have you come to join our staff, Dr. Rush? We need you."

"No—not at this time." Benjamin bent over a man with a bandaged head, "I just came to see—you know I am a member of the Medical Committee of Congress. Perhaps when it learns how things are, the Congress will do something about the Medical Department."

"I pray so," Dr. Smith said wearily. "Things were bad enough when Dr. Morgan was Director General. But at least he did what he could to get us good doctors and sufficient supplies. He never stopped working. But now—well, nobody seems to care any more."

Benjamin straightened up and looked at him questioningly. Dr. Smith lowered his voice confidentially. "Is it true that Dr. Shippen has charge of this area?"

Benjamin nodded. "Yes, he was appointed October last."

"Well, he has been living right here in Bethlehem since December twelfth, but he has yet to set foot in the hospital."

"The devil you say!" Dr. Rush exclaimed indignantly.

It was really too dark to see much of the great Brethren's House now, Benjamin decided. He would return in the morning. Bidding Dr. Smith good night he went out into the village to stay the night with a friend. He inhaled the fresh, frosty air gratefully. How good it was after the fetid atmosphere of the hospital.

On the way to his friend's home he passed a large, imposing house from which came merry sounds of laughter and singing. Since the curtains were not completely drawn against the night, Benjamin could see into a large, handsome dining room blazing with the light of many candles. Around the great table were several couples in fine dress. At their head, raising a crystal goblet of wine in a toast, stood Dr. Billy Shippen.

Anger flooded through Dr. Rush. How *could* Shippen stand there in obvious luxury, drinking and entertaining guests while not a mile away young patriots suffered and died for lack of proper medical care? What excuse could he possibly give for not even visiting the Bethlehem Hospital?

Benjamin wanted to dash through the snowy night back to Philadelphia, rout the Chairman of the Medical Committee out of bed and tell him what he had learned. Then he realized that such action would be useless. Something warned him to go slow, to be sure he could prove his facts first. After all, Dr. Shippen was powerful and charming. He had many friends in Congress, more now than ever since he had triumphed over Dr. Morgan.

Besides, Ben thought hopefully, perhaps things were not as bad as they seemed. Hospitals were always depressing at night. Meanwhile, there was something definite he could do to help the sickness-ridden American forces. He could press for a general inoculation of the troops against smallpox.

This dread disease was rapidly becoming a serious problem as the highly susceptible troops from the southern provinces marched north. Dr. Rush knew that inoculation was not a sure-fire protection, but it helped. In February, 1777, after he had discussed the matter with the rest of the Medical Committee, Benjamin wrote to George Washington.

> The Congress apprehending that the Smallpox may greatly endanger the lives of our fellow citizens who compose the army under your Excellency's command and also very much embarrass the military operations, have directed their Medical Committee to request your Excellency to give orders that all who have not had that disease may be inoculated, if your Excellency shall be of opinion that it can be done without prejudice to your operations.

Washington acted on this suggestion at once. Special inoculating camps were set up in Virginia. Here, soldiers who had never had the disease, stayed for several weeks while they recovered from the mild cases of smallpox which inoculation gave them.

Although the inoculating camps kept smallpox fairly well under control, Dr. Rush noted that after 1777 the American army continued to be plagued by diarrhea, dysentery, typhus, typhoid, measles, meningitis and pneumonia. Malaria was common. Typhus (hospital fever) was the most dreaded of all.

It was disease, rather than wounds, which was feared by both the Revolutionary War doctors and the soldiers. As a medical historian wrote later:

> Hundreds died of wounds which were not at all serious except when made so by the deadly infections against

which no one of the time had any shield. Where bullets killed one, disease killed ten. More surgeons died in proportion to their number than did officers of the line. In every campaign, the army was crippled and hindered by disease.

Dr. James Thacher, a Revolutionary War surgeon, estimated that disease alone had carried off seventy thousand American patriots.

It was indeed a heartbreaking situation, the more disturbing, thought Benjamin, because the British sick and wounded fared so much better. In fact, an American soldier wounded in battle was lucky if he was picked up and carried to the British hospitals. Very likely he would recover.

Of course one reason the British troops were healthier was that they were well housed, warmly clad and adequately fed. They were not like Washington's men who marched bravely across New Jersey in such condition that a British officer wrote, ". . . in the bitter winter the Rebel Army are in so wretched a condition as to clothing and accoutrements that I believe no nation ever saw such a set of tatterdemalions. There are few coats among them but what are out at the elbows; and in a whole regiment, scarce a pair of breeches. Some march without shoes, and most of them are wrapped in their blankets."

Undoubtedly the British soldier was better cared for than the American, but Dr. Rush felt that this factor alone was not responsible for the alarming conditions in the American army. The better showing of the sick and wounded in the enemy hospitals was due in large part, Rush believed, to their following the system of military medicine set forth by their great Physician General Sir John Pringle.

Benjamin knew Sir John well. Years ago in London he had

spent hours in Pringle's house learning about this very thing now so important to the American army—preserving a soldier's health in wartime. In fact Benjamin had nearly memorized Pringle's classic work, published in 1752, called *Observations on Diseases of the Army*.

As he recalled these talks with Sir John, he said to himself, "I believe I could do more to help if I were actually *in* the Army. If I am not re-elected to Congress, perhaps I can join."

Soon afterward, the Pennsylvania Assembly chose a new group of delegates to the Congress, and Benjamin was not among them. "Now I am free to join the Army," he said. He immediately offered his services to the Medical Department.

In April, 1777, the thirty-one-year-old Rush received his appointment. He was named Physician General to the Middle Department—the department which contained the bulk of Washington's army. At the same time he heard that the entire Medical Department was to be reorganized. Who, he wondered with intense interest, would be the new Director General? The post had been vacant since Dr. Morgan's dismissal.

In a few days he found out. The Congress had selected as the Medical Department's new Director General—the genial Dr. Shippen. Although many people wondered at it, Congress, when it appointed Shippen to the post, gave him *all* the power in the Medical Department. He—one man—had no check whatever upon his actions. He was to have complete control, not only over the doctors and medical matters, but over the buying and distribution of all supplies—the foods, the drugs, every single item used in the military hospitals.

When he learned of the new plan of the Medical Department, Benjamin Rush was appalled. What madness was this? One basic strength of the British medical system, he believed, lay in the fact that the doctors attended only to medical affairs.

Special buyers had charge of the foods, drugs and hospital supplies.

With his customary frankness, Dr. Rush lost no time denouncing the new system, both publicly and privately. He was right, and he knew it, but the more indignant he grew, the less tact he displayed. Even his old friends in Congress listened to his remarks with flushes of annoyance.

"We want no system that is like anything British," one congressman told him. "We must avoid open quarrels," said another. "Such dissension only delights and comforts the enemy."

Even Julia couldn't soothe him when he took time off and rode out to Colonel Hall's plantation to see her. They sat in the orchard under a pale mass of pear tree petals.

"Benjamin, Benjamin," Julia said gently, "can you not forget the army hospitals—at least for the afternoon? It is not for you alone to reform the whole department, is it?" She covered his tense hand with her soft one.

"Oh, I know, my dearest jewel," Benjamin answered, his eyes smoldering. "I have always been too quick to speak and to act. But our soldiers die needlessly while Shippen and his friends enjoy the war. Well, Dr. Morgan is not idle. Every day he gathers evidence against Shippen. Perhaps this wastrel will soon be removed. But come, I will speak no more of him. How is my lovely girl? Have you been really well?"

"Yes, wonderfully well," smiled Julia.

From a doctor's point of view, Benjamin wasn't sure. In spite of a determined cheerfulness, she showed strain and nervousness. He knew it was hard for her, this living apart from him, continually fearing for his life and worrying about her father's shattered health and fortunes. He would be thankful when the baby was born—three months hence. Julia would feel less strain then, and so would he.

After he had left his young wife and returned to his hospital post at Princeton, the thought came to him that there was another way in which he could help the sickly American forces. He could, like Sir John Pringle, bring his own knowledge of military medicine to as many people as possible.

There was, he felt, no use asking Director General Shippen to aid with this project. Shippen would never encourage any plan, however worth while, put forth by a friend of Dr. Morgan's. Benjamin himself, however, did not have the money to publish and distribute such information. What then to do?

He decided finally to publish the material in the newspaper, the *Pennsylvania Packet*. This means would cost him nothing, and the information would be seen by everyone of influence, both in the Army and out.

On April 22, 1777, Dr. Rush's piece appeared. It was a long article called "To The Officers in The Army of the United American States: Directions for Preserving the Health of Soldiers." Benjamin clipped the article and sent it to General Nathaniel Greene.

When he received the doctor's paper, Greene studied it carefully. "This article contains information every officer needs," he remarked to his aide. "It should be published as a pamphlet by the Board of War. I shall see what I can do about it." He picked up his quill and scratched off a quick message to Bejamin.

The doctor was overjoyed at General Greene's proposal. This was exactly what he had hoped for. When the pamphlet came out several months later, it contained information which seems simple and obvious to us now, but in 1777 it was a pioneering contribution to American military hygiene.

The pamphlet emphasized the idea, new at the time, that death from sickness in camps is not necessarily connected with a

soldier's life. "The soldier suffers from no different diseases than
does the civilian," wrote Dr. Rush, "but through overcrowding
and lack of simple sanitation, his death rate is much higher."
Unquestionably, Benjamin's arguments for personal cleanliness,
prevention of fatigue and for general sanitation would have
saved many lives had they been more generally listened to.

As it was, *Directions for Preserving the Health of Soldiers*
had tremendous effect. Since it was addressed to the army officers themselves and not to the staff of the Medical Department,
Director General Shippen could not interfere with its circulation. Rush's *Directions* were consulted by army men for many
years. Even as late as the Civil War the pamphlet was twice re-
issued.

On July 17th, word came for Dr. Rush to hurry to Colonel
Hall's plantation. When he reined his horse before the big
white house and raced up the stairs, he found Julia lying in the
airy bedroom, tired but glowing with happiness. By her side,
red faced and pug nosed like any other new baby, lay their son
—already named John. Benjamin bent over the baby with
something like wonder. "Ah, but he is a fine boy, Julia," he said
in a voice deep with feeling. "God has truly blessed us with
such a son."

Many people who thought of Dr. Benjamin Rush as impatient, arrogant and sharp tongued would have been surprised
by the radiance and tenderness on his face.

CHAPTER ELEVEN

Court-Martial

In September, 1777, General Washington's forces were nearly cut to pieces at Brandywine. During the battle Dr. Rush, together with a number of surgeons and surgeon's mates, waited behind a nearby hill for the firing to end. When the acrid smoke had drifted away, Benjamin and his assistants hurried to the battlefield to pick up the wounded. Those badly hurt were carried off in wheelbarrows and on litters, made of poles. The others staggered off on their own feet.

One by one the severely wounded were deposited on the ground in a stable yard close by. Within the stable itself, the surgeons arranged long tables made of doors. Here in a few moments they would begin the amputation of the legs and arms of those whose limbs were shattered beyond healing.

The mates hastily set out the crude-looking knives which the surgeons were to use. They "wasted" no time in washing them. Benjamin had never ceased wincing at the sight of blood and moans of pain. Now he set his mouth and went among the injured men with a reassuring manner. He had to determine which must suffer the dreaded amputation, and which could survive without it. For those who needed to be operated on, he poured out a great dose of whisky to deaden the pain. A week ago he had had a small supply of opium but now this mild painkiller was gone.

He was thankful that the army surgeons were quick, for in

the days before anesthetics, speed was essential in a surgeon. Some of them were not yet deft in tying the blood vessels to prevent hemorrhaging, but all were learning by experience. He could only hope that the turpentine and the weak healing oils the surgeons used would keep the deadly wound infections at bay. It was, he knew, only a hope, because the past record of the healing oils and the turpentine was poor.

The Battle of Brandywine had been fought in early September. By late fall the death rate in the American army hospitals, which had fallen somewhat during the summer, began again to soar. Once more in the improvised hospitals—in the great Brethren's House at Bethlehem, in the burned-out buildings of the College of New Jersey, in the schools and churches of the area, the windows were jammed down tight.

Fires blazed either too hot in the airless rooms, or heat was lacking. In the overcrowded rooms, the helpless patients sweated and chilled. Medicines, proper food, blankets, shirts, clean straw—all were wanting. Soon typhus, pneumonia, influenza and all kinds of infections returned to reach out deadly hands for the undernourished, poorly clothed men.

From his post at Princeton, thirty-two-year-old Dr. Rush watched this development with growing despair. In his own hospital, five hundred men lay in a space suitable for only one hundred and fifty. As a physician, he prescribed the proper drugs and strengthening foods and wines for them, but he soon realized that he was only wasting his time. The patients rarely received these items unless they bought them themselves.

What happened then to the wines and sugar, the fowl and venison, the molasses and other stores he and the other doctors ordered for the sick—and which Congress was now providing? Was it true, as four of the doctors in the Bethlehem Hospital had whispered, that the Director General was deducting one third of all these materials for his own use—to do with as he saw fit?

Could it be, as these same army doctors said, that Dr. Shippen not only took charge of these expensive, hard-to-get necessities, but that he commandeered army wagons to haul them to inn-keepers and others throughout Pennsylvania? And was it a fact that he sold these supplies gathered for the sick and pocketed the money? On his last trip to Bethlehem Rush had tasted the Madeira allowed to the hospital. No question but that it was adulterated and therefore without the beneficial effects of true Madeira.

Benjamin pressed his hands to his eyes. It was too hideous to contemplate. Dr. Shippen couldn't be that indifferent to the sufferers in his charge. No, Benjamin told himself, the fault lay in the system which Congress had mistakenly adopted for the Medical Department. No one man could handle two jobs so enormous. No one man could direct all medical care for the sick, and at the same time serve as purveyor for those supplies.

Naturally, Benjamin reflected, if this person had to account to no one for his actions, he wasn't going to be very accurate in his records. All the European governments understood such a situation and employed more than one man to control health and supply problems. And besides, they made sure that the activities of each officer were checked by and were accountable to other officials.

Benjamin talked over the situation with his colleagues and assistants. Privately, they all agreed with him about the distress in the hospitals. Some of them even violently denounced the sociable, easy-living Director General as the chief cause of the trouble—but that was only in private. Publicly, even the doctors at Bethlehem who had complained about the disappearing sup-plies refused Benjamin's proposal that they all go before Congress and General Washington to try to get the system changed.

Some of them advised Benjamin that he himself would be better off if he would close his eyes to the whole matter. But Benjamin couldn't follow such a course—not when he was by nature sensitive, impatient and conscientious where duty and integrity were concerned. Day after day as he made his rounds in the hospitals he saw the wretched conditions becoming worse. At the same time Dr. Shippen cheerily assured Congress there was no fatal sickness in the army hospitals, and supported his statements by inaccurate and incomplete figures. And all the while Rush noticed hundreds of fresh graves dug in villages throughout Pennsylvania and New Jersey.

By late October while inspecting the hospital at Reading he found the sad state of the Medical Department more than he could bear. "Perhaps," he said to himself, "a letter to John Adams will help."

With a hand so tense that ink sputtered from the quill, he wrote, "Our hospital affairs grow worse and worse. There are several hundred wounded soldiers in this place who would have perished had they not been supported by the voluntary and benevolent contributions of some pious Whigs. The fault is both in the establishment and in the Director General. He is both ignorant and negligent of his duty."

Ten days later—from Bethlehem—Benjamin again wrote Adams, this time even more urgently.

But Adams was too busy to take to Congress complaints sent to him in personal letters. Besides, he had the American morale to consider. Why shake public confidence still further when the Army itself was barely managing to exist through the winter? The families of the soldiers were worried enough as it was. With these things in mind, John Adams kept Dr. Rush's letters to himself.

Meanwhile Benjamin, hating the task, went to Billy Shippen to beg for a more careful allotment of supplies. "Our men die at Trenton and Burlington for want of hospital stores," he stated flatly.

Dr. Shippen was icily polite. He knew what Benjamin Rush was saying about him. He knew also that Dr. John Morgan—with Benjamin's help—was collecting evidence to show that he (Morgan) had been unfairly dismissed from office.

"I shall look into the matter when time permits," he said coldly. "Now if you will excuse me, sir, I have important work to do." He bowed an unmistakable dismissal and left the room.

Two weeks later Benjamin found that the situation in the hospitals was tragically the same. He decided to appeal to another friend in Congress, William Duer of New York.

With a shocked face Congressman Duer read Benjamin's account which ended: "I wish some members of Congress (not related to Dr. Shippen) would visit our hospitals and converse with the principal surgeons in them." But Duer only handed the letter on to another congressman who also did nothing.

Christmas, 1777, was a bleak, miserable day for most of the soldiers in the American army. From the window of a cold, damp church in Princeton which was serving as a military hospital, Benjamin watched large flakes of snow pelt past. He had reached two decisions. The first was that he had only one hope left to get reform in the army hospitals—and that was to put the situation before General Washington himself. His second decision was that if his plea to Washington failed, he himself would resign from the Army Medical Department.

He seated himself at a board which was serving as his desk, took up his quill and began his letter to the General. It was a long letter, right from Benjamin Rush's heart. It described the overcrowding and dangers that existed in the hospitals them-

selves. It told of the lack of discipline among the patients because there were no guards to keep order. It brought out the
risks and inefficiency of the department's organization with its
all-powerful director general. It ended by saying, "If these reforms are carried out, I am sure it will add 3000 men to your
army in the spring who must otherwise perish in our hospitals."

When Washington received Dr. Rush's letter, his own troops
were desperately fighting cold and hunger at Valley Forge.
Every day he saw how his pitiful little army suffered, even when
the men were in good health. How much worse for the sick and
wounded. One thing that Rush mentioned, however, he could
and would do immediately. He appointed a special field officer
to visit all the principal hospitals, and he told this officer to set
up disciplinary regiments at once.

Then he turned Benjamin's letter over to Congress with the
definite request that this body take immediate action upon it.
As a result, Congress which was meeting at York, Pennsylvania, summoned both Benjamin Rush and Billy Shippen to
answer questions.

Dr. Shippen seized the attack. "This man," he said, indicating Benjamin, "wants my job for himself. He neglects his duties
at the hospitals, riding instead about the country stirring up
trouble against me. I refuse to serve with him."

"I would not for all the world have your post," Benjamin
blazed back, white with rage. In his anger Dr. Rush unfortunately was acid tongued and gave the impression of being self-
righteous. Dr. Shippen was as usual charming—and disarming.

Congress listened worriedly to both men. Since they had few
facts at hand, they did not know which one to believe. Many
legislators said frankly they did not know what should be done.

There was no question in their minds, however, that Dr.

Rush's ideas for improving the hospitals were sound. Congress agreed to adopt them. But should they dismiss Dr. Shippen? Well no, they decided—not at present. It would be awkward. He had so many powerful friends. Let him remain as Director General.

Under these circumstances, Benjamin felt that he himself had no choice but to resign as Physician General. One thought, however, comforted him. He had succeeded in getting Congress to reform the Army Medical Department. That was the important thing—the achievement which really mattered.

But, he remembered, there was still the injustice done to Dr. Morgan. Perhaps now that he himself was out of the Army he could actively help the former Director General.

He found Morgan in his Philadelphia home sitting before an empty fireplace brooding over his dismissal.

"I am now ready to ride with you, Doctor," Benjamin said, "and aid in any way I can in collecting evidence."

"My thanks to you, Doctor," Morgan said simply. "Let us start tomorrow."

Together they sought out scores of army doctors and talked to them. Some were willing to give sworn testimony. Many were afraid. But finally, their joint efforts were successful. In June, 1779, two years after Morgan's dismissal by Congress, a Congressional Committee sifted through the evidence the two doctors had collected. The committee then completely cleared Dr. Morgan of all charges of maladministration.

Morgan still felt that this vindication wasn't enough. He couldn't see why Dr. Shippen, the man who had hounded him from the Army Medical Department in the first place, should go completely free and unchallenged—not when the evil results of Shippen's administration were apparent to the humblest surgeon's mate. So he revived his charge of malpractice in the

Medical Department, and demanded that Dr. Shippen be court-martialed.

At last, in 1780, Billy Shippen was brought before a military court. The trial lasted four months and was one of the bitterest in our history. Benjamin Rush and a number of other army doctors presented powerful evidence against him, but once again Shippen was saved by his influential friends. He squeaked through—rescued by only one vote.

The verdict was a curious one. The military court acquitted Dr. Shippen of malpractice, but Congress dismissed him from his job. With the dismissal went the implication that Shippen had indeed been using the hospital supplies for his own profit. A short time later, however, Congress turned around and re-appointed Dr. Shippen as Director General of the new and reformed Army Medical Department. Then after a few face-saving months in office, he was "allowed to resign."

When Benjamin Rush heard of Shippen's forced resignation, he felt only a small satisfaction. "It has come too late in the war," he said, "to be of much value."

For the rest of his life Dr. Rush declared that if the Army Medical Department had been wisely administered, thousands of young patriots who perished would have lived to see their beloved country become the free and independent United States of America.

CHAPTER TWELVE

Doctor to the Nation

When Benjamin Rush resigned from the Army as Physician General, he did not know what to do next. He could not return to his practice in Philadelphia while the British occupied the city. And this was not the time to build a practice elsewhere. Besides—the old doubt had returned to torment him. Should he, he asked himself anxiously, be a doctor at all? Time and again the thought came to him that perhaps he should have followed his own inner feelings years ago and not paid so much attention to Uncle Finley's ideas. He had talked the matter over with Julia's father, at whose shattered home they were now living. What Judge Stockton said rather surprised him.

He was remembering this conversation as he and Julia, with little John toddling by their side, wandered through the peach orchard. Benjamin glanced proudly at his first-born. "What a handsome lad our Jackie is," he remarked for the hundredth time. "How sturdy. What an intelligent brow!"

"Yes, he is the most wonderful baby in the American states," Julia agreed happily. As her dark eyes met the fond twinkle in her husband's glance, they both laughed merrily.

A moment later, Benjamin's gay mood left him. "You do not agree, do you, that I should give up medicine and study law?" he asked in an abrupt tone.

"Well," Julia began cautiously, "I realize father thinks it a fine idea, and I suppose he should know, being a lawyer himself, but you are already a doctor, Benjamin—a very fine one. It seems a pity—" She stopped as she saw her husband's troubled face.

For weeks Benjamin fretted, trying to make up his mind. It would take two years for him to pass the bar. Then he would be thirty-four years old—rather late to embark upon a new profession, even one for which he still yearned.

But then, near the end of June, 1778, the British, afraid that their forces might be blockaded by the French fleet, pulled out of Philadelphia. Behind them, they left so much filth in the streets and in the buildings they had occupied that sickness raged throughout the city.

When Benjamin heard about this situation he felt that it was his duty as a trained physician to help restore the health of this chief city of a desperately fighting nation. "It is clearly my duty," he told himself in a way that permitted no argument. With his mind made up, he saddled his horse and resolutely set out for his office in Philadelphia.

In the years that followed, Benjamin's family increased rapidly. From 1777 when John was born, to 1801 when William, their last baby arrived, he and Julia had thirteen children. Nine of these lived beyond babyhood—a fine record for those days.

During most of these years the big brick house on Walnut Street was crowded. In addition to the children, two servants and a varying number of apprentices, Benjamin's mother and sister Rebecca—now both widows, also lived there.

Of his children, John seemed closest to his heart, although sunny-tempered Emily, brilliant, self-reliant Richard and steady, practical James all brightened his life. At times Julia would take the younger children for a visit with Grandmother

Stockton at Princeton and leave John and Richard with their father.

On one such occasion, when John was nine and Richard six, Benjamin wrote his wife: "I continue to devote a great deal of time to the boys. They ride with me on all my excursions. John has accompanied me three times to the different wards of the hospital. He stood by me and saw a painful and bloody operation performed a few days ago without an emotion."

A week later Benjamin again took John to the Pennsylvania Hospital. Before they climbed the broad steps, the doctor stopped and pointed to a wooden sign which stood near one corner of the red brick building. "Have you ever read this inscription, son?" he asked. "Benjamin Franklin wrote it in 1755 for the hospital cornerstone.

In a clear voice something like his father's, John read aloud:

> In the year of Christ
>   MDCCLV
> George II Happily Reigning
> (For he sought the happiness of his people)
> Philadelphia Flourishing
> (For Its Inhabitants were Public Spirited)
> This Building
> By the Bounty of the Government
> And of many private persons
>   Was Piously Founded
> For the relief of the sick and miserable.
> May the God of Mercies
> Bless the Undertaking.

"Who are the miserable, Papa?" John asked when he had finished reading the sign.

"Well," Benjamin said thoughtfully, "sometimes they are

those who have no money nor any way to earn their living. Mostly though here in the hospital, they are those unfortunates who are mentally deranged. This morning you shall see some of them, for we are going into the mad ward."

Inside the sunny, spacious entrance hall, the steward of the hospital greeted Dr. Rush. "Just look at this fine potato, Doctor," he said, holding up a perfect specimen for Benjamin's inspection. "One of the patients dug it from the hospital garden this morning." Turning to John he said, "Here, young man. You may take this fine vegetable home with you for your supper."

"Thank you, sir," John answered, pleased. A moment later he walked quietly beside his father and the steward down the winding stairs to the basement cells where the "mad people" were confined.

At the first cell, the steward fitted a huge iron key into the lock. Dr. Rush and John stepped inside. By the dim light which filtered through the bars of a small window high above her head, they saw a young woman, rather pretty and refined, sitting on a chair. Her right leg was chained to the floor.

As soon as the girl caught sight of the potato, she stretched out her hands and began to cry and beg for it. The boy unhesitatingly went to her and handed her the vegetable. With an animal-like motion the girl grabbed the potato and stuffed it into her mouth. For an instant it seemed as though she were choking. While Dr. Rush tried to help her, John stared as if petrified. Then with a gasp, he dashed out of the cell, up the winding stairs and out into the sunlight to his father's waiting horse and chair.

He was sitting there trembling when his father, finished with his calls, rejoined him. Then all of a sudden, John was full of questions.

As Benjamin wrote Julia that night:

"He asked me what was the cause of madness, and in particular what was the cause of the poor woman's madness whom we had just seen, and whether it was possible to cure it, how long the disease continued, and whether people have ever died with it. These were his very words. I told him after answering all his questions that he seemed devoted to physic. 'Yes,' said he, 'I will be nothing but a doctor.' I have great pleasure in his conversation upon many subjects."

Benjamin was particularly pleased that John had shown such sympathy with the unfortunate young woman who had lost her mind. Ever since he himself had begun his medical practice, he had been especially interested in the patients who suffered from mental illnesses. That these derangements *were* illnesses of the mind, just as pneumonias and influenzas were illnesses of the body, was a theory of his own upon which Dr. Rush pondered frequently.

At the time he was one of the few people in the world who considered this possibility. Even noted doctors often thought insanity showed possession by the Devil or was a punishment sent from God. The unlucky person who suffered from such trouble was usually hidden by his family, who looked upon his affliction as a disgrace. Frequently he was confined in the local jail where he might be treated like a dangerous beast or exhibited for the amusement of any curious onlooker.

Philadelphia, however, due largely to the wisdom and vision of Benjamin Franklin, had for years shown a more humane attitude toward its insane than had most cities either in America or in Europe. In fact when the Pennsylvania Hospital opened in 1755, a section was set aside for care of the insane.

It was this section, called the "mad ward," that Benjamin Rush made his especial care. From the time that he formally joined the hospital staff in 1783, every day for thirty years—unless he was sick himself, he visited the "lunatics" confined there. From the first day, he observed these patients closely and kept accurate records of the details of their illness. And he did what he could to make their life in the hospital happier and more comfortable.

At this time of his life, however, it was as a distinguished professor of medicine that Dr. Rush was best known throughout the country.

After the Revolution, the medical school of the College of Philadelphia became part of the University of Pennsylvania, and Drs. Morgan, Shippen, Jr., Kuhn and Rush were all reelected to their old posts. Morgan refused to sit on the same faculty with Shippen, and although his chair was kept open for him until his death, he never came back. At first, Benjamin also refused to serve with Shippen, but his friends convinced him that he owed it to the medical students of the new nation to teach them what he knew.

It was awkward having two professors refusing to speak to each other, but in those days it was not unusual. Doctors were often openly bitter in their criticism of one another. Frequently they denounced each other's treatments in letters to newspapers. Sometimes they stood in the back of the room and hissed another doctor's public lectures and experiments. Occasionally they so resented each other's theories that they caned each other in the streets.

Naturally, Benjamin Rush—outspoken, self-assured and quick tempered as he was—had plenty of enemies. But for twenty-five years after the Revolution, even these admitted that he exerted more influence upon the medical profession in America than did any other man living.

During this period he taught over three thousand students.

These students practiced throughout the nation from Massachusetts to Georgia, and they kept in touch with his medical ideas through letters and through his published writings. In this way, for years afterward Dr. Rush's ideas remained their ideas.

In addition to his students, Benjamin also accepted six apprentices each year to work with him in his private practice. One of these apprentices was Elisha Dick, who later became George Washington's doctor. Another was William Henry Harrison, who never practiced medicine. He became instead the ninth president of the United States.

Yet even with six assistants, Benjamin had difficulty caring for everyone who wanted his help. When he arose in the morning, patients were already waiting in his yard. When he opened his front door, he found a batch of notes that had been left during the night, begging him to hurry to the bedside of the sick ones. His office was open until sundown. Then he had a light supper with his family and retired to his sitting room to read, study and write careful case records of every patient.

Sometimes to the busy doctor it seemed that his consultations by correspondence took as much time as did his Philadelphia practice. Sick people from all over the American states wrote, describing their symptoms and begging his help. Often they had no trained doctor available. Frequently they feared that their own doctor was not helping them. Sometimes they enclosed a fee, but more often they did not. Many times they did not even pay the postage for their letters. After a while Benjamin found this postage bill so costly that he refused to accept any letter which came to him postage due.

He never refused, however, the requests which came to him from other doctors, especially from former students. Many asked help which neither he nor any doctor of the time could give.

Such a message was posted from Fredericksburg, Virginia, on

a July morning in 1789. In that little town, George Washington's aged mother lay dying of cancer of the breast. Her physician Dr. Hall hoped Dr. Rush would know of some new cure. "Was," Dr. Hall asked, "Dr. Martin's celebrated cancer powder of any value?"

Benjamin knew all about Dr. Martin's cancer cure. As a chemist he had carefully tested it, as he had tested many remedies. "No," he wrote back immediately. "Martin's powder consists largely of arsenic, and is of no use in treating cancer. "In fact," Benjamin told his inquirer, "there is no cure for cancer except the knife—used early."

With his huge practice and his teaching, many Philadelphians thought Dr. Rush must be rich. But actually, as his family increased, he grew poorer. For one thing, inflation was running wild in the United States. American money lost value from day to day. Often by the time the patients paid their bills, the money was worth so much less than when Benjamin had treated them that the payments were worthless. Besides, he treated many patients free—including all ministers and officers of the Revolutionary War.

Other doctors, too, were concerned by the distress which the post-Revolution inflation and unsettled business conditions had brought to Philadelphia. One of these was a kindly little Quaker named Samuel Griffits.

"I know not where the sick poor can turn now," Dr. Griffits said to Benjamin one snowy day in the winter of 1785. "The Pennsylvania Hospital has not the proper funds for them, and although thee does all thee can, and I, too, it is not enough for these worthy people."

"I know," said Benjamin thoughtfully. "What Philadelphia needs is a free public dispensary—a place where the poor may come for free treatment, and for medicines without charge also. Of course the doctors would have to donate their services, but you and I do that anyway, and I am sure that others will, too."

" 'Tis an excellent idea," Griffits said enthusiastically, "if we can but raise money for a building, medical equipment and drugs."

Money. The obstacle was always money, Benjamin thought ruefully. How now could he raise funds for the free clinic? The answer came to him in Philadelphia's love for lectures. Perhaps he could persuade Dr. Moyes, a famous blind scientist who was visiting the city, to give a public lecture and donate the proceeds to a dispensary fund.

Dr. Moyes agreed to give the talk, and Benjamin with his usual energy set about rounding up a large audience. The lecture not only raised some immediate money for the clinic, but it also brought in enough contributions so that on April 12, 1786, Drs. Rush and Griffits were able to announce in the *Philadelphia Packet*:

> The Philadelphia Dispensary for the medical relief of the poor will be opened this day at 12 o'clock in Strawberry Alley.

This dispensary was the first free medical clinic in America, and to it Benjamin Rush devoted many years of unpaid service. The dispensary very shortly proved its worth, for during the first five years of its existence, nearly eight thousand patients received treatment there.

One day a year later Benjamin paid his usual visit to the "mad ward" at the hospital. On this particular morning he was worried about a thirty-year-old patient named Johan Dingle. Three weeks ago when Dingle had been brought to the hospital, he was in a maniacal state of mind, although he was strong and well physically.

Now he lay on a pallet of straw in his basement cell, feverish and coughing with a lung fever. This sort of setback happened too often, Benjamin reflected unhappily. He had seen many "lunatics" restored to normal living by kind and understanding treatment, nourishing food and healthful surroundings. Few of the deranged patients in the hospital, however, received this kind of care. They might not suffer the stigma of being confined in a pail, but physically they were not much better off.

Perhaps, Benjamin thought, if the managers of the Pennsylvania Hospital understood the situation, they would change it. With this hope in mind he wrote them the following letter.

Gentlemen: Under the conviction that the patients afflicted by madness should be the first objects of the care of a physician at the Pennsylvania Hospital, I have attempted to relieve them, but I am sorry to add that my attempts, which at first promised some improvement, were soon afterward rendered abortive by the cells of the Hospital.

These apartments (rooms) are damp in winter and too warm in summer. They are moreover so constituted as not to admit readily of a change of air; hence the smell of them is both offensive and unwholesome.

Few patients have even been confined in these cells who have not been affected by a cold in two or three weeks after their confinement, and several have died of consumption in consequence of this cold.

These facts being clearly established, I conceive that the appropriating of the cells any longer for the reception of mad people will be dishonorable both to the science and humanity of the people of Philadelphia.

Should more wholesome apartments be provided for them, it is more than probable that many of them might be relieved by the use of remedies which have lately been discovered to be effectual in their disorder.

With great respect, I am, gentlemen, your friend and humble servant,

Benj. Rush

At the time that Dr. Rush wrote the managers of the hospital, letters were treated with dignity and great consideration. Thus when the managers received Benjamin's communication, they conferred among themselves. Then they sent for him.

"We are in deepest sympathy with your appeal, Dr. Rush," they told him, "but we simply cannot spare more rooms in the hospital for the deranged. We have too many other patients to care for. If there are to be more rooms for the mad patients, there will have to be a larger building. And that takes money."

Money again, the forty-two-year-old doctor thought wearily. Then he said, "As you know, gentlemen, I have but little time for such things, but I will see what I can do."

For five years he worked at this task. He spoke to public gatherings on the need for better care for the deranged. He published articles on the subject in the newspapers, and he personally visited members of the State Legislature and explained the need to them.

By February, 1792, Benjamin Rush had won a real victory. The State Assembly passed a bill appropriating the money for the construction of a special wing for "the accommodation of the diseased in body and in mind."

Benjamin was so pleased with this success that he decided he could relax a bit. First he took Julia and the girls to see a fierce two-year-old lion which was on exhibition in Race Street. Then he had breakfast with his good friend Thomas Jefferson. A few days later he took an evening off to visit with James Madison.

As good Republicans, the two men spent their time praising the Republicans and Tom Jefferson and condemning the Federalists and their leader Alexander Hamilton.

Although when he resigned from the Army Medical Department Benjamin had declared that he was through with politics, he really wasn't. Actually, he spent hours every month writing to John Adams about every angle of American politics. Adams, of course, was a strong Federalist but these two signers of the Declaration of Independence had long ago developed a friendship that was above political party.

About this time, Benjamin noticed that his twelve-year-old son Richard was developing a real interest in law and politics, and he was pleased. He didn't find Richard, who was a top-ranking student at Woodbury Academy, much of a problem. But John was something else.

John Rush, his father had to admit, at fourteen was over sensitive, hot tempered and irritable. He had two loves—his gun and his flute. Benjamin didn't approve of John's spending much time with either, but he considered the flute the lesser of two evils.

One day just before John was to leave for his studies at Princeton, Benjamin called him into his book-lined sitting room. Julia was there, too, her head bent low over a small tapestry, but as usual where John was concerned, it was Benjamin who did the disciplining. The doctor looked up at his tall, brown-haired son and said sternly,

"You may continue to play your flute, John—if you will promise to give up your gun."

"All right." The boy's sullen tone annoyed his father. Perhaps Benjamin thought, I had better let him know that he will be as closely watched at college as he is at home.

"One more thing, John," Benjamin continued. "I wish to

read to you from the letters I have written Professor Minto. Since you are to stay with him, you may as well know what we expect of you there." He placed his steel-rimmed spectacles on his nose and read:

"Dear Professor Minto—You will oblige me by taking charge of our son John and superintending his morals as well as his studies. I shall expect that he will *study* constantly in your house and never enter the College except when he goes to say his lessons or perform some academical exercise. On no other condition can I consent to sending him to Princeton, for I consider a *college life* and *college society* to boys of his age alike fatal to morals and manners.

". . . John's temper is a little irritable, but he is as easily governed as a child when he sees a due degree of authority over him. He inclines to be idle, but by a little attention, he can be made to spend whole days in study."

Benjamin did not notice John's scowl, and his own face softened at the final words of his letter.

"For every attention paid to my boy, you will ever find Mrs. Rush and myself truely grateful; being our first-born, he is in some measure the *spes gregis.*

The *"spes gregis"*—the hope of the flock. It was a large order for a fourteen-year-old boy to fill. Silently, without a glance at either of his parents, John left the room. A few minutes later Benjamin heard the sweet rippling sounds of the flute coming from the boy's bedroom.

The doctor sat on the arm of Julia's chair. "John must derive his love of music from you, my dear," he said affectionately.

"True he is a strong-willed, wayward lad, but of fine quality, and wanting only constant discipline. I love him dearly."

Julia's lips smiled at her husband, but her eyes were troubled.

Four months later Dr. Benjamin Rush abruptly removed his son from Princeton. John had, in his father's view, inalterably disgraced himself. His crime was playing cards for money—upon the Sabbath. In accordance with the rules at Princeton, John and his partners had to confess their wickedness before the whole college assembled for evening prayers. "Our first-born son in such a situation! It is almost too cruel a blow to bear," Benjamin told Julia through tight lips.

"I wish I knew what to do about John," Julia agreed when the boy arrived home—unusually quiet and subdued. "He *is* difficult. Obviously he is of high intelligence, but he is full of moods. Perhaps he works too hard."

"Works too hard!" Benjamin snorted. "Nonsense. He doesn't work hard enough. Remember what Uncle Finley always said —'Idleness is almost a sin'? In any case, 'tis time John prepared for a profession. He has always said he wished to be a physician. So beginning tomorrow, dear Julia, I shall prepare John to become my apprentice."

CHAPTER THIRTEEN

Panic in Philadelphia

Almost a year later, on a cloudy August morning in 1793, Dr. Rush stepped briskly out of his red brick home and frowned. Another hot, sticky day. When would Philadelphia get relief from this steaming weather which for weeks had been weakening its inhabitants and bringing out swarms of annoying insects?

His neat green suit was damp with perspiration as he hastened toward the waterfront to visit Mrs. Peter LeMaigre. The condition of the streets made him frown even more. The open gutters, dry from lack of rain, were filled with smelly refuse of all kinds.

Perilous, that is what it is, Benjamin thought. Plain perilous. All over the city now were these stinking piles of waste throwing out on the air their poisonous effluvia. And to make matters worse, the long dry spell had produced new marshes and stagnant pools where once pleasant streams had been.

Benjamin was certain that this stagnant water was also throwing out its poisons. For years he had tried to interest city officials in keeping the land in and around the city well drained, but few people thought this was important. After all, anyone living in a low, flat town like Philadelphia had to expect these stagnant pools from time to time.

As usual these last weeks, the doctor noticed that the streets were filled with French refugees. These newcomers had fled from the revolution in the sugar-growing island of Santo Domingo (Haiti). Many of them, he heard, had been carried from

137

the escape ships half dead with a mysterious fever. But so far as he knew, the native Philadelphians had not as yet shown similar symptoms.

Still there was a strange sickness about. Just yesterday his friend Peter Alston had died of an odd, violent disease. It had come on him suddenly. When Benjamin arrived, he found Peter sitting on the bed, clammy cold all over, with his face a peculiar yellow. Benjamin had promptly prescribed the strongest cordials, but his friend died in a few hours.

Then there was young McNair whose body was covered with an eruption which puzzled Benjamin. Actually, this eruption looked very much like mosquito bites, but of course they couldn't be, he decided. They must be the deadly petechiae which accompanied many fevers and were always an ominous symptom.

Now his quick step brought him into the narrow, crowded little alley near the Delaware, called Water Street. At No. 77 he sounded the brass knocker of the LeMaigres' house. The LeMaigres weren't his patients, but their own doctor, Dr. Foulke, had asked them to call in Benjamin for consultation. Dr. Hodge, the LeMaigres' neighbor, was there, too.

When he saw the patient, Dr. Rush's heart sank. Poor Mrs. LeMaigre was gasping for air. A great heat, she said was burning in her stomach. Her yellow face looked pleadingly toward the doctors for help.

Benjamin pulled a chair toward the bed and smiled encouragingly at the desperately ill woman. "Now let us see what is going on," he said in a reassuring tone. But it was too late. Catherine LeMaigre was already dying.

Shortly afterward, the three doctors gathered sadly outside the house. "There has been an unusual number of bilious fevers about lately," Dr. Foulke remarked—"of uncommon malignancy."

"Aye," agreed Dr. Hodge with vigor, "this mortal disease has already carried off five people within sight of this very door —my own sweet little Jane among them."

Benjamin Rush listened thoughtfully. He had already noted that his own patients with this deadly illness lived in this very neighborhood. He was finding it hard to breathe. Some stale, powerful smell choked his lungs.

"What is that dreadful odor?" he asked weakly.

"Oh," Dr. Hodge raised his hands in disgust, " 'Tis that rotten coffee from the sloop *Amelia*. It rotted on the voyage, and the crew dumped it on Ball's wharf in the next square. 'Tis been there a month, decaying more every day."

"Where did the sloop come from?" Benjamin asked.

"Santo Domingo. It was near to sinking, so crowded it was with refugees and that stinking coffee. Many of the refugees were sick, too."

Dr. Rush stiffened. The effluvia from that rotten coffee! That was where the poison was coming from. Every person sick with this dreadful fever must have inhaled the noxious substances thrown into the air by that rotting coffee on Ball's wharf.

The trouble was, Benjamin reflected, that now it was too late. Even when the coffee was hauled away, the victims of the fever were already giving the horrible disease to others. What was this disease? Benjamin had had his suspicions for some days now, but he was almost afraid to name it. As a matter of fact, he had not seen this awesome killer since 1762—over thirty years ago when he was a young apprentice. He had almost forgotten it—almost, but not quite.

Out of this frightening memory of the past, Benjamin spoke in a voice tight with feeling. "I fear, gentlemen, that bilious remitting yellow fever is now abroad in our city."

Yellow fever. The dread disease! The other doctors' eyes flared wide in dismay.

For a while they stood together in silence, thinking. They were good doctors for their time, but they were working within the darkness of ignorance. Even years later when doctors did know about germs, bacteria and insect-borne diseases, the cause of yellow fever remained a puzzler. Most medical men still believed it was contagious. As late as 1897 yellow fever still carried off hundreds of people in our coastal cities like New Orleans. As a matter of fact, it was not until 1900 that the disease was conquered, for in that year the heroic United States Army doctor Walter Reed and his volunteers showed that yellow fever was carried from person to person by a certain kind of mosquito.

At first in 1793 not everyone accepted Benjamin's diagnosis. Some doctors scoffed at the idea. The illness was nothing, they said, but a severe form of the usual Autumnal Disease. Rush was merely trying to stir up trouble. But if there *was* a serious fever around, it must have been brought in by the Santo Domingan refugees or other immigrants. Quarantine all ships from the sickly regions, these men declared, and the disease would be stopped at the source.

This argument touched off a battle between the doctors and real estate agents and others who were afraid that if Philadelphia got the name of being a "sickly" city, land values would fall and business would suffer. Congress itself might decide that Philadelphia should no longer serve as the nation's capital, as it was supposed to until 1800. Then the prosperous port of trade, the elegant, cultured city of fifty-five thousand people would become little more than a country town on the waterfront.

With Dr. Rush's reputation, however, his opinion could not be ignored. Soon a number of other doctors agreed with him that the fever, although it may have been brought in from time to time, was now local in origin. Clean up the filth of the city, they said. Remove the heaps of garbage near the city market. Drain the marshes and the swamps. Cover up the great open sewer on Dock Street. Do all these things, and the putrid miasmas which were rising from these places would disappear.

In a way they were right—Benjamin and the doctors who agreed with him—even though they did not know why they were right. Draining the marshes and the swamps and covering the open sewers would have greatly cut down the breeding places of the disease-carrying mosquitoes. Perhaps such measures, taken in time, would have prevented the great horror which now began to sweep relentlessly throughout the city.

With sickness springing up everywhere, Benjamin scarcely had time to talk with his mother and sister who were taking care of household matters while Julia and the younger children visited Grandmother Stockton in Princeton. He managed, however, to keep an eye on the three older boys—James, Richard and John—who ran from him to keep from breathing in the poisonous miasma from his clothes.

Fortunately, his Negro servants Marcus and twelve-year-old Peter went ahead with their work—fever or no fever. His five apprentices, too, he thought gratefully, were hard working and intelligent, especially young Johnny Stall whom Benjamin loved as much as he did his own sons.

Even though his house was overcrowded with people, the doctor missed Julia intensely. No matter how exhausted he was, he saved a few minutes every day to write to her.

On August 25th, he wrote:

My dearest Julia,
    Since my letter of Friday the fever has assumed a most alarming appearance. It not only mocks in most instances

the power of medicine, but has spread through several parts of the city remote from the spot where it originated. Water Street between Arch and Race streets is nearly desolated by it. In one house I lost two patients last night —a respectable young merchant and his only child. His wife is frantic this evening with grief.

Five other persons died in the neighborhood yesterday afternoon and four more last night at Kensington. Many people are flying from the city, and some by my advice. Pray for me, dear Julia. I enjoy good health and uncommon tranquillity of mind. While I depend upon divine protection and feel that at present I live, move, and have my being in a more especial manner in God alone, I do not neglect to use every precaution that experience has discovered to prevent taking the infection. I even strive to subdue my sympathy for my patients; otherwise I should sink under the accumulated loads of misery I am obliged to contemplate. You can recollect how much the loss of a single patient once a month used to affect me. Judge now then how I feel in hearing every morning of the death of three or four.

The next evening Benjamin wrote Julia that he had had to pack John, Richard and James off to an uncle in Trenton. They were so afraid of picking up the infection, he said, that they were becoming nervous. Besides, they complained of headaches.

For a moment the doctor laid his quill across the silver inkwell and sat thinking. In her last letter Julia had wanted to know more about the dread disease itself. Just what could he tell her? He picked up his quill.

The doctor stopped writing and raised his head to listen to the tolling of the church bells. It seemed now as if they never stopped their doleful ringing for the dead. He shook his head. The church bells ought to be silenced. They sent an already nervous people into a panic. With a sigh, he went back to his letter.

Johnny Stall, my apprentice, sleeps and eats with us, and thereby relieves us very much. My mother and sister are part of the means that Providence employs to preserve me from the infection. My sister has contrived a small mattress on some chairs on which I rest myself by lying down every time I come into the house.

He sealed his letter and then left in the rain for the small brick building of the American Philosophical Society near the State House. Here the College of Physicians were meeting to decide what could be done about the alarming epidemic. Only sixteen of the twenty-six doctors were able to attend. Old Dr. Redman, the president, was calling the meeting to order as he entered.

The doctors talked for hours but they got nowhere. There were always the same arguments. The disease was local in origin. It was not local but brought in from abroad. What would prevent this deadly and, as they thought, contagious fever? No one knew. Benjamin shifted restlessly in his chair. Clearly the meeting was a waste of time.

He agreed, however, to write the report which was to be published in the newspapers as advice to the citizens. This report, a combination of the opinions of all the physicians of the college, gave only general advice such as avoiding fatigue, drafts, the evening air, sick persons and filth. It advocated the use of vinegar, camphor and burning gunpowder to "purify the air."

The publication of the "Physicians' Report" only alarmed the people more. Now that the doctors themselves admitted a strange epidemic was about and indicated they didn't know what to do about it, many people became afraid to go outside, even to draw water from the pumps.

They stayed indoors, scouring, whitewashing and "purifying" their houses by burning gunpowder, tobacco and niter. They sprinkled vinegar through every room. Those who did go out carried as protection a piece of tarred rope or a camphor bag. They chewed garlic and poured vinegar on themselves constantly. Since tobacco was supposed to be a disinfectant, almost everyone smoked. Even women and children went around with cigars in their mouths. As a further sanitary measure, the Governor ordered a company of militiamen to draw a small cannon through the streets, stopping every few yards to fire it.

Friends stopped shaking hands. Often they pretended not even to "see" acquaintances, for after all, who could tell? Perhaps at the very moment the acquaintance might be falling sick with the dreaded fever. People walked down the middle of the street to keep as far away as possible from contaminated houses.

Within a few days, almost all normal business processes stopped. There were few people around able or willing to carry out the simplest duties. No one could be hired to carry away the trash and garbage. So many seamen were sick that ships could not be unloaded at the wharves, and there was no room at the docks for incoming vessels. All kinds of supplies grew scarce.

The schools closed because teachers and pupils were sick or had fled the city. Banks closed and cash was hard to get hold of. There was no one to handle the mail. Letters were dumped at the University of Pennsylvania, and people picked them up as best they could. Citizens were no longer even sure what time it was because there was no one to fix the clocks and watches. One night the City Watch cried "Ten o'Clock" when it was really only nine, but few people seemed to know the difference. Nor did they care.

So many city officials fell sick or had fled that civil government itself began breaking down. Now there seemed practically no one left to take responsibility for the deserted sick. Mayor Clarkson remained at his post and did what he could with the few helpers available. There was a great need for some place to care for the deserted sick and for the sick poor who could afford no care.

Since there was no such place, these poor and abandoned people were picked up and carried to an enclosed amphitheater known as Rickett's Circus. There they were placed on the ground and left to die alone and without care. Later, a large mansion on the edge of the city, called Bush Hill, was made into a yellow fever hospital, and these unfortunates were taken there.

A sort of insanity born of fear seized Philadelphia during the first few weeks of the epidemic. The slightest symptom—a mild cold or a simple headache—was looked upon as the dreaded disease. Sometimes in their hysteria, husbands deserted sick wives, and wives locked their husbands out of the house to be sick in the street. Some terrified parents even abandoned their children, and children fled from their ill parents, leaving them helpless in their misery. Finding food became a problem because farmers refused to bring their products to the infected city.

And day after day Dr. Rush noticed huge swarms of mosquitoes buzzing about in the damp heat. Some old-time Quakers thought these pests were another affliction which God had sent to punish an arrogantly rich and pleasure-seeking city.

Although outwardly he was cheerful and confident, inwardly Benjamin was sunk in depression. Everywhere he met only tears and silent grief. Aside from the funerals which passed by in silence and lonely haste, the deserted streets were ominously still. One day a two-year-old child smiled at him, and he was startled by the happy expression.

Late one night he sat in his study searching desperately through his medical notes. A sudden breeze swept through the open window, making the candle flicker, then flare. In its uneven light, the doctor's thin face showed white and drawn with fatigue. From the street he heard the slow, creaking wheels of the wagons of the dead. More yellow fever victims, he thought, being carried like so many logs to be tossed into a common grave.

Benjamin buried his face in his hands. "God in heaven, help our desolated city," he prayed in anguish. He was tired, very tired. How could he think when his brain seemed merely an aching lump in his head?

Yet he had never really given up hope. There must be a cure for this fever—there must. He believed that God always provided a cure for every illness. It remained only for man to find it. But what—what would defeat this yellow killer?

He had tried everything he knew. The gentle purges, and the mild bleedings, the recommended cool air, the cold drinks, the low diet, and the cold baths of the French doctors. He had given the bark in all its usual forms. He had applied blisters to the limbs, the neck and the head. He had tried to rouse the system by wrapping the whole body in blankets dipped in warm vinegar. He had rubbed the right side of the patient with mercurial ointment in an attempt to rouse the liver. But his patients still died, their tortured faces begging him for the help he so fervently wanted to give.

He rested his eyes for a moment, then continued his search. One manuscript still remained to be read—an old folio which Benjamin Franklin had given him years ago. It had been written by Dr. John Mitchell, an English physician and naturalist who had observed a yellow fever epidemic in Virginia in 1741.

Suddenly as Benjamin's eyes took in the script, a shock of understanding rocketed through his feebly working brain. What was Dr. Mitchell saying? He was saying that an *ill-timed scrupulousness about the weakness of the body on the part of the physician was fatal to the patient.* Dr. Mitchell had fought the terrible fever with the strongest measures possible. He had fought it as though he were fighting the Devil himself, and in the same spirit. Fight fire with fire. Fight weakness with weakness.

It was true, Dr. Rush knew, that in this dreadful disease the abdominal viscera were often filled with blood. In his manuscript, Mitchell had emphasized that to rid the body of the poisonous matters—the deadly humors which filled the whole system—the most powerful bleeding and purging must be done, and *done immediately*. Don't take the weakness of the patient into account at all, Dr. Mitchell warned. Because he is so weak, he cannot assist nature to evacuate the poisonous matter— Thus the doctor must do it for him.

Benjamin paused in his reading and stared thoughtfully into space. "A new train of thought broke in upon my mind," he wrote later. "Doctors ever regarded their efforts as merely assistant to nature, yet Mitchell blandly proclaimed that the physician must domineer over nature.

Like other doctors, he had set out to strengthen—not weaken, to restore—not tear down. Yet he had lost his patients. True, he had already used purges and bleeding, but mild ones, and they had failed. Could it be that weakness should be made weaker, after Mitchell's fashion?

In the wavering candlelight, Mitchell's words seemed to the exhausted physician to be written in words of fire. Boldness— that was the weapon. Boldness never before known in bleeding and purging.

A great fatigue stole over Benjamin Rush. When had he rested except for a few moments on a pallet thrown over two chairs in the kitchen? He couldn't even recall his last meal. Just a little broth and milk. That was all he had had for days. His head dropped on the desk and he slept fitfully.

Then at dawn he awoke with a start and remembered that he had to go out on his rounds. What was it he had been read-ing in that old folio? Oh, yes, Dr. Mitchell had saved his patients by a mighty bleeding and purging.

Now the strongest purge Dr. Rush knew was the one he had used in the Revolutionary War—ten grains of mercury (calomel) and ten of jalap. It was an enormous dose even for a strong young man. What would it do to a patient already seri-ously weakened by yellow fever? Benjamin didn't know. He was afraid to think. *But Dr. Mitchell had written*, "An ill-timed scrupulousness about the weakness of the body is often fatal to the patient."

"I'll try it," Benjamin muttered to himself. "After all, I have tried everything else."

CHAPTER FOURTEEN

End of the Plague

His first call was to a man alone in a closed house. The patient was at the point of death, clammy and yellow. His family had fled without leaving him even a cup of water. If he himself did nothing, Benjamin knew, the man would surely die. And any well-known remedy he might use probably would not save the patient either. What was there to lose, he asked himself, if he tried Dr. Mitchell's method?

Nervously Benjamin forced the oversized dose of mercury and jalap down the man's throat. Then from the weakened body, he withdrew several ounces of blood. After that, he sat with the patient to wait until the drastic purge emptied the man's bowels. It wasn't long. The patient was so weak from the ordeal that he could scarcely keep his eyes open. But almost immediately, Dr. Rush observed, he began to recover.

The doctor then tried the violent "cure" on three other seemingly hopeless cases. They also got well. Benjamin was overjoyed. Although he didn't understand how his "cure" worked, he was certain he had found a way to defeat the yellow killer.

He began stopping other doctors in the street and telling them about his treatment. He presented his views to the College of Physicians. In order to reach more people he published directions for bleeding and purging in the newspapers. Such directions, he thought, might save persons who could not quickly secure a doctor.

149

Of course, many patients he treated died. But when this happened, Dr. Rush believed that the treatment had not been started early enough. Or perhaps the treatment had been too mild.

Some doctors agreed with Benjamin's extreme treatment. Others didn't. But none of them knew what they were fighting or how to fight it. Underneath their professional calm their hearts beat as bewilderedly and as helplessly as those of the most ignorant patients.

As Philadelphia sweltered through the hot days of early September, a number of doctors themselves sickened. Many ran away. Nobody knew where Dr. Shippen was. Dr. Kuhn, who had caught the disease early and recovered, fled to Bethlehem, Pennsylvania. From there he wrote violent letters to the Philadelphia newspapers denouncing Dr. Rush who was working over eighteen hours a day trying to help his patients.

That he *was* helping them, Benjamin never doubted for an instant. A serene confidence marked every feature of his intellectual face. When they saw this look of confidence and faith, and when they learned that here was a doctor who would offer hope and warm sympathy no matter how tired or busy he was, the desperate Philadelphians flocked to his office. They blocked his chair in the streets and begged him, sometimes on bended knee, to try to save their loved ones. Those who could, offered him large sums of money to visit their families, but Benjamin gave his services to rich and poor alike.

His five apprentices moved into his home, and together with their master, they saw people at all hours. Even while he ate, patients were admitted, interviewed and had mercury and bleeding prescribed.

But despite the efforts of Benjamin and of Dr. Devize and other French physicians (who used a milder treatment), the deaths mounted. Soon it became impossible to find anyone to attend the sick. At the beginning of the epidemic, only a few white nurses had been available. Now most of these were either sick or had fled.

This situation brought more worry to Dr. Rush. In his opinion, nursing care was as important to recovery as bleeding and purging. But if there were no nurses, what was he to do? There were, of course, the Negroes—about twenty-five hundred freedmen in Philadelphia. They were completely untrained. But why, he asked, couldn't they be instructed in the care of the sick—especially since they themselves were immune to this horrible sickness?

In 1793 most doctors thought that Negroes were immune to yellow fever. And in the beginning of the epidemic, this indeed seemed to be the case, for during the first month, no Negro was known to have had yellow fever.

In all America, the Negroes knew they had no better friend than Benjamin Rush. They knew that he had published one of the earliest pamphlets against slavery. They knew that he had given hours of labor and money to help them build a fine church of their own. Of the Philadelphia Negroes, three especially were regarded by Benjamin as his friends. These were Richard Allen, William Grey and Absalom Jones, all of whom were officials in the Free African Society—an organization founded by the Negroes themselves to help sick, widowed or fatherless members of their race.

To these three friends Benjamin said, "Since God has granted you special exemption from the disease, will you not see what you can do to help the stricken white citizens of Philadelphia?" He also published his appeal in the newspapers.

The Free African Society responded immediately. Yes, their members, poor and uneducated as they were, would do whatever they could to help in this dread plague. Jones and Allen called on Mayor Clarkson and asked how the Negroes could be of most use. These men were the first volunteers in Philadelphia to offer their services to the city.

It was decided that the Negroes would tour the stricken city on foot, street by street, alley by alley, to look for the helpless sick and dying. When they found such sad cases, they were either to carry them to Bush Hill, or they were to find nurses from their own number for them. Sometimes these searchers were too late. Then they put the bodies into rude coffins and carried them to the graveyard.

As the unusual steaming heat continued, however, it was clear that the Negroes were not immune to the yellow killer. They, too, sickened and died with frightening suddenness. But most of those who remained well watched their heroic leaders Jones, Gray and Allen plod along, bravely following the doctor's directions, and they stayed in the fight with them.

By the middle of September, the epidemic was worse. The despairing people watched well over one hundred burials a day. Now all who could tried frantically to flee the city. The roads leading from Philadelphia were crowded with refugees, but most of them could find nowhere to stay.

People were afraid to give them food and shelter. Sometimes armed guards turned them back as they tried to enter another town. Even Secretary of the Treasury Alexander Hamilton and his wife, who had recovered from the fever, were not allowed to enter New York state until a committee of doctors from Albany had sailed across the Hudson to examine them.

By the middle of September, Benjamin himself fell sick. For weeks he had been sleeping only three hours a night. It was an effort to drag himself out of bed in the morning. But he never thought of giving up, even though Julia wrote him a frantic letter begging him to save himself.

Late one night he found a patient who needed immediate bleeding. It was too late to send for a bleeder so Dr. Rush undertook the task himself. The exertion overheated him, and he shivered driving home in the cooling night air.

By dawn he knew he was running a fever. He called an apprentice and had him withdraw ten ounces of blood from his arm. Then, believing he was better, he called for his chair and visited nearly fifty cases. Somehow he got through the morning, but when his friend Mr. Mervin, the schoolmaster, died after piteously begging Benjamin to save him, it was too much. The sick and anguished doctor stumbled out to his chair and sobbed like a child.

Back home he was seized with another violent chill. Was it the yellow fever, he asked himself? But what else could it be? He sent for Johnny Stall and John Coxe, his favorite pupils, and placed himself in their care. They bled him and purged him—and he slept.

Three days later, Benjamin crept downstairs, sat weakly in his parlor and prescribed for over one hundred people.

On September 19th he resumed his visiting. His cheeks were still flushed with fever, and a cough frequently shook his thin frame. When he had to visit patients in an upstairs room, he got there by clinging to the banister and pulling himself up step by step. Often he was so dizzy that he lay down beside the patient for a few moments. Sometimes it took a sip of wine or milk to revive him. But he never gave up hope. He never turned away one patient if he could manage to see him.

While Benjamin fought his own illness, the pestilence struck the other members of his household. Kind-faced, conscientious Johnny Stall fell ill. Dr. Rush put him to bed in the back

bedroom and asked Fisher and Coxe to look after him. Then
Fisher was stricken. John Alston, a third apprentice, collapsed
in his rooming house, and Warner Washington, his fourth
apprentice, lay burning with the fever at his lodgings a few
blocks away. Soon sturdy John Coxe drooped. The Rush house
was like a hospital. Benjamin, his sister Rebecca and his
seventy-two-year-old mother all tried to take care of the apprentices, as well as attend the hundreds of people who clamored
for attention.

In this dark moment Benjamin did not have even the help
of his trusted servant Marcus whom the doctor had trained to
mix powders, spread blisters, and give clysters, for now Marcus
was sick, too.

When his sister Rebecca and his mother both began to com-
plain of chills and headaches, the doctor felt he could bear no
more. Of all the household, only the twelve-year-old servant
boy Peter remained well. "Peter has become to us a little host,"
Rush wrote Julia that night. "He is not only useful to us in the
family, but has this evening visited two patients for me." The
patients were glad to see Peter, for in their despair anyone
connected with Dr. Rush carried a measure of hope with him.

With his mother and sister drooping, and the apprentices
ill, Dr. Rush gratefully accepted the help of the two untrained
Negro nurses the Free African Society sent to aid him. They
did what they could, but the yellow killer was merciless. First,
Warner Washington died. Edward Fisher's life hung in the
balance for days, but he recovered. John Coxe, too, was able
to conquer the fever. With mounting helplessness, however,
Benjamin watched his "dear and amiable pupil" Johnny Stall
sink below hope.

A day later nineteen-year-old Johnny died. He had been
writing to his father as he lost consciousness. Benjamin read

the fragment of the unfinished letter. "You must excuse me, Father," Johnny had scrawled, "for not writing you, as I am doing good to my fellow creatures. At this time, every moment I spend in idleness might probably cost a life . . . so many doctors are sick, the poor creatures are glad to get a doctor's servant." Dr. Rush had loved the boy deeply. He put the scrap of paper away and treasured it for the rest of his life.

But sorrow had not left the Rush household. So tired he could hardly scribble, Benjamin dashed off a note to Julia. "Scarce had I recovered from the shock of the death of this amiable pupil (Johnny Stall) when I was called to weep for a third pupil. On the 24th my dear boy Alston expired."

Benjamin stopped writing and raised his head hopefully at the swirl of the curtain in a sudden, damp-smelling breeze. His quill went to the paper. "Thank God, not only for my life and health, but for the appearance of the weather. An equinoctial gale with rain would do more for our city than a thousand physicians."

But the looked-for gale did not come. When the next day's sun rose brassy in the sky, things were even worse for Dr. Rush and the stricken city.

He had managed to get through his morning calls by frequent pauses on the stairs and occasional sips of milk and wine, now his only nourishment. Then at noon he went home. With fever-flushed face, John Coxe met him at the door.

"I am terribly sorry, sir," Coxe said, "but I can no longer remain on my feet. And your sister has taken to her bed. Your mother, too. I'll return when I can." He swayed slightly as he closed the door behind him.

Benjamin hurried to his sister's room. "Rebecca," he said anxiously, "are you feeling very ill?" His heart contracted as he saw the deadly yellow already spreading over her face.

Rebecca managed a wan smile. "I'm sorry, Benjamin," she whispered, "when you need me so much. But see to mother."

His mother sat propped up in bed, her eyes glittering with fever. She wasn't, however, Dr. Rush observed thankfully, seriously ill. He was sure she would recover.

He crept wearily to the back parlor and in spite of himself gave way to gloom and despair. A small sound at the door made him lift his eyes. The servant Marcus, out of bed for the first time, had crawled from the laboratory and come to the parlor door. Benjamin bade him come in and sit by the fire but, wrote the doctor later, "he added by his silence and dullness to the gloom which suddenly overpowered every faculty of my mind."

For several days Rebecca "hung over the grave by a single thread of cobweb." Afraid to leave her for long, Benjamin dashed out in his chair to see what patients he could, then returned hurriedly to his dismal household.

But in spite of his care, his sister Rebecca died of yellow fever. She was, Dr. Rush wrote in his journal, "a martyr to the cause of humanity."

In the days that followed, his mother, John Coxe and Edward Fisher all recovered, but Benjamin's own strength was nearly at an end. On October Fourth he fainted in the sickroom of a patient. He could no longer eat. Every movement was painful. A week later, he was again seriously ill—this time definitely with yellow fever.

As Dr. Rush lay fighting for his life, the plight of the stricken city grew even worse. At the height of the plague, it was estimated that six thousand out of fifty thousand people were ill of the fever at the same time. The few doctors who had not fled grew more frantic as they grew more tired. Desperately they switched back and forth from one treatment to another.

One group of doctors, angered by Benjamin's confident and stubborn claim that his was the only helpful treatment for yellow fever, denounced him as a senseless bleeder who was murdering his patients.

Hurt and bewildered, Benjamin Rush fought back against his critics. They were, he declared, jealous of him. In a way this may have been true, for no other doctor received such public blessings as he did. "Rush is become," a noted Philadelphia judge wrote at the time, "the darling of the common people, and his humane fortitude and exertions render him deservedly dear. Fugitives drink his health, and prayers for him ascend from congregations all over the country."

Actually, from what we now know of the value of a good blood supply, it is difficult to understand how anyone could live through Dr. Rush's tremendous bleedings. Yet there must have been something about his faith and optimism—his clear trust in the love of God—which pulled so many of his patients back to health. Perhaps the unswerving firmness with which he gave his treatments, and the hope and courage he imparted to others were even more healing than his methods were destructive.

When Benjamin was well enough to leave his home and go about the city visiting patients, he was struck with the different look of the streets. The air was crisp and healthfully cold—too cold for the deadly mosquito, although nobody thought about that. More people were in the streets, and many of them were plump and rosy, smiling and relaxed. They must be fugitives returning to their homes, he thought. How different they looked from the skinny, yellowish, scared-looking persons who scurried through the streets during the height of the plague.

How busy and strangely full of plans for the future they

seemed. How quickly forgetful of the thirty-five hundred of their fellow citizens who had died in the horrible epidemic. But this, the frail doctor realized, was only natural and human. Why, he thought joyously, soon Julia and the children will be returning to the big brick house on Walnut Street. Then, as he too felt the stirrings of a life ahead for him, he smiled in the pale October sunshine.

It was, however, another month before Benjamin deemed the dread epidemic to be truly over and allowed his family to come home.

CHAPTER FIFTEEN

The Problem of John

After his exhausting labors in the yellow fever plague, Benjamin made a real effort to relax. One of the things he enjoyed most was horseback riding in the country with Julia. One soft spring afternoon in May, 1794, when they returned home from a ride along the Schuykill, John raced out of the doorway waving a letter.

"It's come, Father," he called excitedly—"my commission as ship's surgeon aboard the *Scimitar*. We sail for Calcutta in a fortnight. Isn't that splendid?"

An expression of relief crossed Benjamin's face, and he glanced swiftly at Julia. They were both worried about John, because obviously something was wrong with him. Just what, neither could tell.

For months now, the boy had been restless and unhappy and seemed to be suffering "an obstinate, slow remittent which threatened consumption." Since a long, slow sea voyage was the usual prescription for this ailment, Benjamin had recommended that John apply for the post of ship's surgeon. Of course the seventeen-year-old boy was no graduate doctor, but the small ships of those days were glad to sign on even partially trained men as surgeon.

Now as Dr. Rush caught the answering spark of approval in his wife's eyes, he said, "Excellent, son. In honor of the

159

occasion I shall present you with a fine mahogany medicine chest."

John Rush was at sea for nearly three years. In the spring of 1797 he came home, looking tanned and cheerful, apparently eager to resume his medical apprenticeship with his father. By late summer, the young man's services were really needed, for yellow fever again struck Philadelphia.

Fortunately the cases were neither as severe nor as widespread as in 1793. But once again the same arguments flared among the medical men. None of them, including Benjamin Rush, seemed to have learned a thing from the nightmare autumn of four years ago.

Still convinced that bleeding and purging had been the most effective treatment against the disease, Benjamin went back to this method. As before, some doctors sided with him; others, against. But since the situation was nothing like as desperate as in 1793, citizens did not panic and die by the hundreds. This time Benjamin did not stand out as a hero. He was just another doctor trying to do his best against yellow fever.

But in the fall of 1797, as an aftermath of this lighter epidemic, a strange factor entered the fight—one which nearly destroyed Benjamin Rush.

It began one morning in October as the Rushes were eating breakfast. Suddenly John, who was reading the *Gazette of The United States* called out angrily, "Have you seen this article, Father?"

Benjamin's mouth tightened, but he said in a level voice, " 'Tis nothing new, John, for me to be denounced in Fenno's paper. After all, he is Colonel Hamilton's (Alexander Hamilton) protégé, a Federalist of marked stripe. He dislikes me for my Republican principles."

" 'Tisn't that." John rose abruptly, upsetting his coffee cup.

"This article impugns your medical skill. It calls you an un-principled quack. A murderer who has killed thousands by the lancet and bleeding cup." John's eyes were pale with fury. "The article is unsigned, but I know who wrote it—Dr. Andrew Ross. I will take care of him," John muttered in an ominous voice as he dashed from the room.

Several days later a letter signed by John Rush appeared in another Philadelphia newspaper. It defended his father and denounced Dr. Ross as an incompetent muddlehead. Unfortunately, that very day Dr. Ross and John met each other in Prune Street. "You impudent puppy," Ross snapped.

For a moment John only stared angrily. Then in a gust of rage he brought his cane down on the older man's head. White faced and shaking, Dr. Ross picked up his fallen hat and stamped away.

That afternoon, Dr. Andrew Ross challenged Dr. Benjamin Rush to a duel.

Benjamin was heartsick at John's behavior, but he declined to fight. "Not because I fear death," he told Dr. Ross, "but because I do not wish to answer to my Maker for causing another man to be a murderer."

The unsigned articles and letters in Fenno's newspaper abusing Benjamin were distressing enough. But they did not compare in invective with the ones which were appearing at the same time in another Federalist paper called *Porcupine's Gazette*. This gazette was edited by a peculiar, colorful, brilliant young man named William Cobbett, or as he signed himself, Peter Porcupine.

In his native England, Cobbett was known as a firebrand, and as one of the most savagely satirical writers his country had ever produced. He was still an English citizen and an ardent Royalist who had never forgiven the colonies for winning their

independence. He hated, he proclaimed in his maliciously
amusing way, all Republicans, especially that "great Republican
quack, that bleeding, purging signer of the Declaration of
Independence—Dr. Benjamin Rush."

Just why Cobbett seized upon Benjamin as the public target
of his hate is not clear since the doctor was no longer active
in politics. Of course it was known that Rush was the friend
of the outstanding Republican—Vice-President Thomas Jefferson. But he was even closer to the nation's foremost Federalist
—President John Adams. Cobbett, on the other hand, was a
warm friend of Alexander Hamilton's who, although also a
Federalist, disliked Adams intensely. And since Hamilton also
disliked Benjamin and disagreed publicly with his medical
theories, some people thought it was Hamilton who encouraged
Cobbett to attack Rush. It was an indirect way they said, by
which Hamilton could "get at" President Adams.

Whatever the cause, Cobbett's cruel but humorous shafts
against Dr. Rush gave Philadelphians the most fun they had
had in years. Forgotten were Benjamin's years of unpaid service
to the poor, his services to—and reforms of—the Army Medical
Department during the Revolution. Forgotten were his courage
and self-sacrifice during the yellow fever epidemic. Overlooked
were the thousands of students he had inspired, the humane
care and the hope he was giving to the mentally ill. Whenever
Porcupine's Gazette appeared, the citizens hurried to buy it and
laugh over such notices as the one titled "Rush and His
Patients."

Wanted by a physician, an entire new set of patients,
his old ones having given him the slip: also a slower
method of dispatching them than that of phlebotomy
(bleeding), the celerity of which does not give time for
making out a bill.

Even in an age when public abuse was common, Cobbett was going too far. Benjamin knew that in another few months his practice, his good name, the happiness of his family, all —would be completely destroyed. Even now, John went around with a frightening grimness, and the younger children were mocked at school and in the streets.

Much as he disliked the idea, Benjamin decided to take Cobbett to court on the charge of libel. In December, 1797, the case of Rush vs. Cobbett came to the State Supreme Court, but it was two years before it was actually tried.

Meanwhile, Dr. Rush's practice, from being the greatest in the nation, dwindled to practically nothing. For a time no new medical patients, except a few West Indians and other foreigners, came to him. He still had his classes at the University, but these, too, had shrunk in number. Also, it took a tremendous effort to maintain his dignity before his students who naturally were reading Peter Porcupine's comments with relish. Things got so bad for Benjamin and his large family that he applied for a government job at the mint—a job he had once disdainfully turned down.

When President Adams selected him as the best qualified of the forty applicants for the position of Director of the Mint, the doctor was not only grateful but relieved. It was a good job for him as it took only two hours a day. He held it for the rest of his life.

One March day in 1798 Benjamin sat alone in his office. He looked too thin, and at fifty-two his hair was almost completely gray. As he ruefully recalled how crowded with patients this same office used to be, the thought came to him that perhaps this state of affairs was a blessing in disguise. Now that his time was not taken up with the ordinary sicknesses, he could devote more attention to the deranged.

And heaven knows, he reflected, these poor, unhappy, misunderstood creatures need attention. How few human beings there are who will give them even sympathy. How few doctors will bother with them.

While he was thinking, a carriage stopped outside his gate, and a middle-aged man stepped down and held out his hand to a woman heavily covered with a veil.

"Another deranged person," Benjamin decided as he observed the woman's stiff movements. As was his way with such patients, he went to meet them with a kindly smile.

"Doctor," the man said, when he and his wife were seated in Benjamin's office, "I am Campbell Morrison—from Georgia. I have heard that you have had uncommon success in restoring the deranged. My wife, she—well—" Morrison turned a distressed look toward the unnaturally silent woman."

"I understand," Benjamin said gently. "It appears that your wife suffers from a tristimania. I believe she can be made well again."

"Oh, do you really think so, Dr. Rush?" the man asked in a voice deep with relief.

Benjamin nodded. "Yes, six months ago a youth in like condition was brought to me from Massachusetts. He is now home and at work. A sickness of the mind is like a sickness of the body. Often it can be healed by kind and understanding care, nourishing food, clean, cheerful surroundings and ample rest. But not too much rest," he emphasized to Morrison who was hanging on his words. "The patient must be kept busy with such simple labors as will keep him healthfully occupied."

This matter of simple labors, or occupational therapy, as it is called today, was one of the great reforms which Dr. Rush introduced into the treatment of the insane in America. On April 30, 1798, he wrote the managers of the Pennsylvania

Hospital, "Certain employments are to be devised for such of the deranged people as are capable of working. Spinning, sewing, churning, etc. might be contrived for the women. Turning a wheel, particularly grinding Indian corn in a hand mill for the horse or cows of the hospital, cutting straw, weaving, digging in the garden, sawing or planing boards, etc, would be useful for the men."

In the same letter Benjamin also requested that the managers install two bathrooms—one with hot water, the other with cold, for the use of the patients. "Such baths," he wrote, "have a soothing effect upon the mad people." In those days there was no running water. The baths were showered down from tanks attached to the ceiling.

Whether the patient was under private care or an inmate of the Pennsylvania Hospital, Benjamin made careful notes on each case. It was clear to him that not all mental derangements were the same or had the same cause and the same cure. Whenever some thought or observation struck him as significant, he entered it into a special notebook called "Diseases of The Mind." He was always on the lookout for experiences other doctors the world over had had with this type of patient.

Once he wrote Jefferson asking to borrow a book the latter had bought in Paris dealing with the experiences of a former madman in a French asylum. "For several years past," Benjamin's letter said, "I have been engaged in investigating the causes, seats and remedies of madness and other diseases of the mind. Before I commit the results of my inquiries and observations to the press, I wish to read everything that has been published on these subjects."

Perhaps, he thought as he sealed the letter, such a book will help thousands of patients whom I can never see.

Occupied as he was with his insane patients, his book on

Diseases of the Mind, and his teaching, Dr. Rush was able to ignore the continuing jibes of Peter Porcupine. John, however, now found life in Philadelphia unbearable, and one spring day in 1798 he went to his father's office.

"Yes, John?" Benjamin deftly poured a quantity of James Powder into a bottle.

"Father," John said abruptly, "Tomorrow I leave to join the United States Navy. I can bear it here no longer. There is no place for me as surgeon."

Benjamin eyed his son intently. The boy's drawn face showed strain. "Perhaps it is best, John. The sea is ever good for a restlessness of spirit."

John remained a surgeon only a short time. A year later he became a lieutenant in the Navy.

By December, 1799, Benjamin was able to write his oldest son some good news. The case of Rush vs. Cobbett had finally come to trial. The jury had found William Cobbett guilty of libeling the doctor with many untrue accusations. He was ordered to pay Benjamin five thousand dollars and the costs of the trial.

The verdict of the jury was a bitter pill for Cobbett to swallow. In fact, it ruined him. His Philadelphia property fell under the sheriff's hammer, and the sheets of part of a new edition of *Porcupine's Collected Works* were sold as wastepaper. Benjamin, still neat and elegant in his threadbare coat, took the money Cobbett eventually paid over to him—and donated it to charity.

But unfortunately for the doctor, the trial did not end Cobbett's abuse. Instead, the eccentric journalist grew even more vitriolic. As he left Philadelphia for New York, he announced in a loud voice that his "sole motive had been to expose the menace to Philadelphians' lives that lay beneath Rush's sleek-headed, saint-looking appearance."

Then he scribbled a letter to a close friend in the British Legation. "Nothing provokes me but the thought of such a whining Republican rascal putting the five thousand dollars in his pocket. . . . The villain shall not enjoy his prize in peace. I shall find the means of reaching him be I wherever I may."

Cobbett's means of "reaching" Rush proved to be an even more vituperative publication than *Porcupine's Gazette*. It was a little magazine called *The Rush-Light*, and every word of its contents was devoted to a savage, witty abuse of Dr. Benjamin Rush.

Benjamin read the first issue of *The Rush-Light* in a daze of bewilderment. Was Cobbett mad? If so, his madness had the cleverness of the Devil. What should he himself do now?

As he held the magazine in his shaking hand, Julia stepped into his study. "Benjamin," she said gently, trying to keep the distress out of her voice, "word has come—Richard is in trouble."

"Richard!" The magazine dropped from his hand. "How? Where is he?"

"Well, right now, he's in the Mayor's Court. Dr. Glentworth has brought charges against him."

"What do you mean?" Benjamin felt he couldn't be hearing correctly.

"I'm afraid it is that dreadful Cobbett again," Julia replied evenly. "After Richard read what Dr. Glentworth is supposed to have said about you, he sought out Dr. Glentworth in his surgery—and soundly thrashed him."

"Oh, Julia, no!" Benjamin sank back in his chair. "Not Richard. Why in all his nineteen years he has been as calm as a rock. Now if it were John—" his mouth tensed. "I only hope, my dear, that John never sees this damnable pamphlet."

But the doctor's hope was in vain. The very day that Richard Rush assaulted the prominent Dr. Glentworth, Lieutenant John Rush unexpectedly came home on leave. There was no hiding *The Rush-Light* from him. John read the poisonous remarks concerning his father with an ominously still face. Then on the back page, he came across something about himself.

"I affirm," Cobbett had printed, "this John Rush to be an impertinent puppy, a waylaying coward, a liar and a rascal."

John flung the magazine to the floor. "I am taking the first mail stage to New York," he shouted, his eyes blazing. "When I finish with that villain, he will never write another lying word." He angrily threw off his father's restraining hand and dashed out of the house.

Luckily, before the mail stage reached New York, Benjamin, by hiring a special express rider, got word to a friend in that city. The friend stationed himself at Cobbett's door, and managed to lead John away before the young man had a chance to attack the journalist.

In all, Cobbett brought out five scurrilous issues of *The Rush-Light*. Then in June, 1800, he sailed back to England. Not only Benjamin Rush, but all the Republicans were glad to see him go.

For awhile after Cobbett left, life was peaceful and sunny for Dr. Rush and his family. The new nation he loved was thriving. Over five million people now lived in America, a gain of over a million since the first census was made in 1790. The national capital had been moved from Philadelphia to Washington, an event which didn't interest Benjamin as much as what Benjamin Waterhouse, a young doctor, originally from Boston, was doing on a nearby Philadelphia street. With

Thomas Jefferson's assistance, Waterhouse was trying out a new method of fighting smallpox. It was called vaccination.

Benjamin's own family was thriving, too. Julia, at forty, still had the slender grace and gentle look of her girlhood. John seemed content with his life in the Navy. Emily, twenty-one, was happily married to a rich young Canadian, and Richard at twenty was establishing a reputation as a lawyer. Sixteen-year-old Mary, sweet tempered and pretty, and fourteen-year-old James, preparing for Princeton, were, in their father's opinion, "ideal children." The three youngest Rushes—Benjamin, Julia and Samuel—all were happy, healthy and bright.

By December, 1802, however, an ominous cloud appeared over this peaceful scene. John was again unhappy.

"I want to come home, Father," John's letter read, "and resume the study of medicine. Rather than continue to follow a sea life, I will become one of your men servants or even clean your stable."

This time Benjamin thought John had better enroll as a medical student at the University of Pennsylvania rather than serve as apprentice to himself.

John did well at the University, and in June, 1804, he received his degree of Doctor of Medicine. But then, oddly enough, he decided not to practice. Instead, he accompanied Major Pierce Butler, the senator from South Carolina to his southern plantation and stayed there a year. After that John rejoined the United States Navy, first as a sailing master, then as the commander of a gunboat.

All this instability worried Dr. Rush, but he knew it would be foolish to try to force his son to practice medicine. Such a doctor would only be harmful to his patients. After all, Benjamin reflected, John was now thirty years old and responsible for his own life.

Two years later, on a clear October day when the leaves were crimson on the oak tree in his garden, Dr. Rush received word that his son John had killed another naval officer in a duel at New Orleans. Because of this, the letter said, John was under arrest.

Benjamin heard that Lieutenant Turner, the officer killed, had been John's best friend, and that John hadn't wanted to fight him at all—especially over some trivial argument. But Turner had insisted. He had called John a coward for refusing to fight, and had declared that he would either "kill or be killed." So John had agreed to the duel.

The naval officers in charge must have decided that John was not to blame because a few weeks later he returned to duty as commander of the gunboat. But John, his father soon realized, was not able to dismiss the incident from his mind. He grew irritable and depressed. The letters he wrote home brought only distress to his parents.

Perhaps this is why in July, 1808, when Benjamin received a call to attend the man he disliked most on earth—Dr. Billy Shippen—he went with a more understanding heart. Dr. Shippen, although wealthy, lived with sorrow in his great Germantown mansion. Of his eight children, only two had reached adolescence. Then Thomas Lee, his only surviving son, handsome, brilliant and lovable, had died early of a consumption. At the same time his once beautiful wife and his lovely daughter Nancy lived hidden away in the darkened rooms of the vast house—victims of a religious mania.

Benjamin saw immediately that Dr. Shippen, suffering from anthrax, was beyond hope. He did what he could, but two days later Billy Shippen died.

With a somber face Benjamin wrote in his Commonplace Book:

This day at 6 o'clock in the evening died at his seat near Germantown, aged 72, Dr. William Shippen. . . . He retained his reason but not his speech to the last hour of his life. . . . Over his faults, etc, let charity cast a veil. He was my enemy from the time of my settlement in Philadelphia in 1769 to the last year of his life. He sent for me to attend him notwithstanding, in his last illness, which I did with a sincere desire to prolong his life. Peace and joy to his soul forever and ever.

When he finished writing he sat quietly, thinking. Then with a sad shake of his head, he flipped back the pages of his notebook to read what he had written in October, 1789.

This afternoon I was called to visit Dr. Morgan, but found him dead in a small hovel, surrounded with books and papers, and on a light dirty bed. He was attended only by a washerwoman, one of his tenants. What a change from his former rank and prospects in life! The man who once filled half the world with his name had now scarcely friends enough to bury him.

Three months after Dr. Shippen's death, tragedy struck the Rush family. Its shadow first appeared in the form of a letter from John. There had been more quarreling and gunplay aboard his ship, he wrote. As a consequence he had been removed from his ship and was being sent to Washington for investigation.

Some weeks later, Benjamin and Julia felt better. A letter from John told them that the unfortunate matter had been cleared up and that he was back at his post in New Orleans.

But in March, 1809 came a letter from Captain David

Porter. "Your son John has tried to take his own life," the letter read. "I regret to tell you that he is deranged."

"Deranged!" His beloved John for whom he had had such great hopes. Dr. Benjamin Rush shook his head unbelievingly.

A few minutes later when Julia came and put her arms around him, the doctor buried his face in his hands and wept without restraint.

CHAPTER SIXTEEN

The Father of American Psychiatry

After Captain Porter's letter came, Benjamin and Julia Rush sat a long time in the darkening study, holding hands and trying to comfort each other. At last the doctor roused himself. "Come, my dearest," he said, forcing a cheery tone. "This is no way for us to behave. It is evident from what Captain Porter writes that John suffers a melancholia, brought on by that duel. A melancholia can be healed."

At the time of Porter's letter, John was already in the Marine Hospital at New Orleans. At first it seemed that he was recovering, but after a year, the doctors there gave up hope and sent him to Washington where he was discharged from the Navy.

In February, 1810, John's nineteen-year-old brother Ben, and old William, Dr. Rush's faithful Negro servant, journeyed to the federal city and brought him back to Philadelphia.

Ben led his brother from the carriage into the wide entrance hall where Benjamin and Julia had hurried when they heard the carriage wheels. "Here is John, father. He—he," Ben choked and fled up the stairs.

The days that followed were sharp with anguish for the Rush family. Julia tried to busy herself with household affairs, and Benjamin, pretending eye trouble, avoided seeing either patients or friends. After a while he wrote to James who was completing his medical training at the University of Edinburgh:

> Your brother John arrived in a state of deep melancholy. Neither the embraces nor tears of your mother, father, sisters, nor brothers could obtain a word nor even a look from him. His countenance is pale and discovers (reveals) no marks of his disease being induced by any other cause than by the death of his friend by his hand in 1807.
>
> This evening we conveyed him to the Hospital where all its officers vied with each other in offers and promises of kindness to him. To your parents this sight and this close and intimate union with his woes have been truly distressing. Your mother mourns, but it is with the resignation of a Christian. I do not despair, with the medical resources of the Hospital, of his recovery.

And later to John Adams Benjamin wrote more fully:

> John arrived in Philadelphia in a state of deep melancholy and considerable derangement. His long and uncombed hair and his long nails and beard rendered him an object of horror to his afflicted parents and family. No entreaties could induce him to utter a word to any of us. After three days spent in unsuccessful attempts to alter his appearance, we sent him to the Pennsylvania Hospital where he has been ever since.
>
> . . . . Could the advocates for duelling and the idolators of the late General Hamilton peep into the cell of my poor boy, they would blush for their folly and madness in defending a practice and palliating a crime which has ren-

dered a promising young man wretched for life, and involved in his misery a whole family that loved him.

With John confined to the "mad wing" of the Pennsylvania Hospital, Benjamin naturally took an even greater interest in the treatment and comfort of the mentally ill.

Every day as he made his rounds in the hospital, he looked in on John just as he did the other patients. The young man was getting better, the doctor judged. He now took an interest in his appearance and spoke to his father and the hospital staff. Still, Benjamin realized, it would be some time before anyone could tell how permanent John's improvement would be.

Although John did not need to be confined in a strait jacket, many of the violent patients did. Benjamin thought this restraining device was unnecessarily cruel and devised a strapped chair which he called a "Tranquillizer." He had other practical suggestions, too, all of which he took to the managers of the Pennsylvania Hospital and asked that they be tried out on the patients.

It was the custom of the day to put such requests into long letters called "Memorials." The Memorial Benjamin wrote to the Hospital managers in September, 1810, is considered so remarkable by present-day psychiatrists that on the strength of these suggestions alone, they designate Dr. Benjamin Rush as the "Father of American Psychiatry."

This historically important memorandum emphasized points Benjamin had made earlier. Through the years he had observed that a mental patient who was getting well could lose ground if he were placed with patients in a violent, noisy stage. So now he asked for separate buildings for "patients in the high and distracted state of madness."

Because Dr. Rush placed great value upon the dignity of every human being, no matter in how pitiful a condition, he asked that no one except the hospital staff be allowed to "converse with or even see the Mad People without an order from the attending physician. Too many mentally ill people who might be cured," Benjamin commented, "refuse to go to a hospital because they fear they will become public spectacles— as unfortunately they do throughout most of the world."

Through the years also, Benjamin had observed that idleness only made mental troubles worse. Therefore he again insisted to the Hospital managers, as he had ever since 1798, that every patient who was able to work—whether plowing, or sawing wood, spinning, weaving, painting or writing—should be made to do so.

Benjamin had noticed, too, that patients often improved if they could talk at length to their physician about their troubles. If they did not wish to talk, sometimes they could be led to write out their disturbing thoughts, and this, too, seemed to help them. With this in mind, Dr. Rush asked the managers to appoint an "intelligent person" whose special job it was to converse with the patients and "read and write upon subjects suggested from time to time by the attending physicians."

When Benjamin had finished writing the actual recommendations in the 1810 Memorial, he pushed his small steel spectacles back on his high forehead and thought for a few minutes. Then with a sigh he picked up his quill and continued:

There is great pleasure in combatting with success a violent bodily disease, but what is this pleasure compared with that of restoring a fellow-creature from the anguish and folly of madness, and of reviving in him the knowledge of himself, his family, his friends and his God?

But where this cannot be done, how delightful the consideration of suspending by our humanity their mental and bodily misery! Degraded as they are by their disease, a sense of corporeal pleasure, of joy, of gratitude, of neglect, and of injuries is seldom obliterated in their minds.

Again Benjamin paused. The memory of his own unhappy son pacing back and forth in the hospital garden came to him. Sorrow lined his face as he wrote:

I shall conclude this letter by an appeal to several members of your board to vouch for my having more than once suggested most of the above means for the recovery and comfort of the deranged persons under your care long before it pleased God to interest me in their adoption by rendering one of my family an object of them.

I am, gentlemen, with great respect and esteem, your sincere friend and servant,

Benjamin Rush

The managers of the Hospital adopted most of Benjamin's suggestions, although it was several years before they could raise the money for some of the improvements.

During these years, although Julia felt that with John's illness some of the sparkle had gone from Benjamin, to most of his acquaintances he seemed the same. The only change they remarked upon was that his hair, which he wore hanging to his coat collar, was now a soft, silky white. He still fixed his large, brilliantly blue eyes upon his students and greeted them with a courteous bow and a firm, "I hope you are very well today, sirs." He still walked briskly and held his slender, graceful figure erect in a neat suit of drab gray-green. And as always, he entered the sick room with quiet reassurance and understanding sympathy radiating from his scholarly "alive" face.

But inwardly Benjamin felt as though he was always hurrying through his other duties to get to the book he was writing on diseases of the mind. His book—that was the important thing in his life now. Many times these days the earnest face of Uncle Finley rose before his mind's eye, and he fancied he could hear the positive voice declare, "It is with the study of physic, Benjamin, that you will help mankind."

Well, he hoped his book would help mankind. In any case, the sixty-seven-year-old doctor told himself, it would most assuredly bring a larger understanding of the mentally ill themselves. Absorbed as he was in this volume, he was scarcely aware of the honors which came to him because of his previous writing and teaching. The French Academy of Medicine made him a member. And the Russians were so impressed with his medical studies that their doctors elected him to the Imperial Academy of Sciences, and the Czar sent him a diamond ring.

Then at long last, in November, 1812, *Medical Inquiries and Observations Upon the Diseases of the Mind* was published. Benjamin inspected the small brown, leather-covered volume with a thrill of accomplishment. One copy, fresh off the press, he sent to John Adams with this accompanying note.

The subjects of them (diseases of the mind) have hitherto been enveloped in mystery. I have endeavored to bring them down to the level of all the other diseases of the human body, and to show that the mind and body are moved by the same causes and the same laws.

Of course many of Dr. Rush's "cures" were later found to be worthless, and his basic premise that mental illness is usually a disease of the blood vessels in the brain was later disproved. Modern psychiatrists, however, give him credit for introducing three great advances into the treatment of the insane.

First —he advocated occupational therapy.

Second—a century ahead of his time, he advised that the patient talk and write out his tensions with his physician.

Third —he produced one of the first systematic works on diseases of the mind written in the western world.

Diseases of The Mind—now called a distinguished pioneer study—was used for fifty years as a standard reference work by doctors and medical students in America and in Europe. Not until 1883 did another comparable systematic work on insanity appear.

Benjamin Rush lived only six months after *Observations on Diseases of The Mind* appeared in print. In April, 1813, the weakness in his chest, which had plagued him all his life, became acute. Julia anxiously called his physicians Drs. Dorsey and Physic. They hurried to his home and bled him and fed him wine whey. But Benjamin only grew weaker.

A few days later Julia sent for Richard, who was living in Washington and already being spoken of as the next Attorney-General of the United States. John, unfortunately, was still too cloudy in mind to leave the hospital.

At dusk on April 19th, Benjamin reached for Julia's hand. Then with a direct glance at his son Dr. James Rush, he whispered, "Be indulgent to the poor."

Those were his last words.

After he died, doctors and important people on both sides of the Atlantic wrote and spoke in praise of Dr. Benjamin Rush. In the American states, Former President Jefferson said, "Another of our friends of '76 is gone, another of the cosigners of the Independence of our country. And a better man than Rush could not have left us, more benevolent, more learned, of finer genius, or more honest."

And Former President John Adams said, "As a man of science, letters, taste, philosophy, patriotism, religion, morality, merit, usefulness taken altogether, Rush has not left his equal in America, nor that I know of in the world."

These words of John Adams—"usefulness taken altogether"— are the key to Benjamin Rush's whole life. He was above all a *useful* man.

As a doctor and as a chemist he used the poor science of the time to help literally thousands of people. He brought more healthful conditions to the Revolutionary War soldier, and he helped establish the first free medical clinic in America.

As a teacher, he brought knowledge and inspiration to thousands of medical students.

As a patriot, he helped publish *Common Sense*. He served as Physician General during the Revolution, he was a member of the Second Continental Congress, and he signed the Declaration of Independence.

As a psychiatrist, he made perhaps his greatest contribution. In this field he was a true pioneer, bringing proper treatment and hope to hundreds of patients otherwise doomed to live in mental darkness.

He was, in short, one of those Universal Men—like Thomas Jefferson and Benjamin Franklin, who lived in our country when such energetic, learned, broad-visioned and humane citizens were most needed—the time when the United States was born.

Bibliography

Bettman, Otto L. *Pictorial History of Medicine,* Charles Thomas, Publisher, Springfield, Illinois, 1956.

Brown, Harvey E. *The Medical Department of the U.S. Army from 1775 to 1873,* Washington, Surgeon General's Office, 1873.

Drinker, Cecil K. *Not So Long Ago.* Oxford University Press, New York, 1937.

Duncan, Louis C. *Medical Men in the American Revolution, 1775-1783.* Medical Field Service School, Carlisle Barracks, Pa., 1931.

Flexner, James Thomas. *Doctors on Horseback,* Garden City Publishing Co., Inc., New York, 1937.

Goodman, Nathan G. *Benjamin Rush, Physician and Citizen,* Philadelphia, University of Pennsylvania Press, 1934.

King, Lester S. *The Medical World of the Eighteenth Century,* University of Chicago Press, Chicago, 1958.

Packard, Francis R. *History of Medicine in the United States,* Vol 1, P. B. Hoeber, Inc., New York, 1931.

Powell, John H. *Bring Out Your Dead,* University of Pennsylvania Press, Philadelphia, 1949.

Ruschenberger, W. S. *An Account of the College of Physicians of Philadelphia,* W. J. Dornan, Philadelphia, 1887.

Rush, Benjamin. *The Autobiography of Benjamin Rush*, Edited by George W. Corner. Princeton University Press, Princeton, 1948.

—— *The Letters of Benjamin Rush*, Vols. 1 and 2, Edited by L. H. Butterfield, Princeton University Press, Princeton, 1931.

—— *Observations on Diseases of The Mind*, Philadelphia, 1812.

Shryock, Richard H., Editor, *One Hundred Years of American Psychiatry*.

Woodward, W. E. *The Way Our People Lived*. E. P. Dutton & Co., New York, 1944.

Index

Index

187